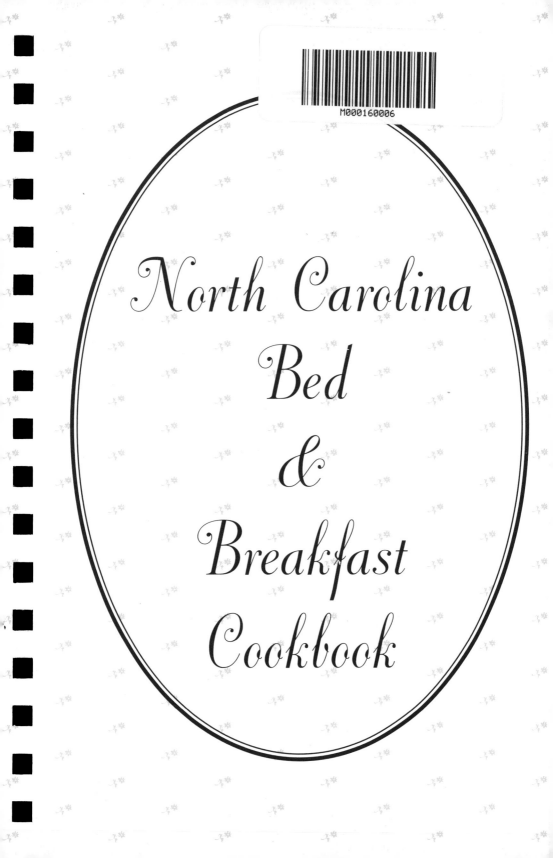

North Carolina Bed & Breakfast Cookbook

North Carolina Bed & Breakfast Cookbook

First Edition

ISBN 1-889593-08-7

Printed in China

Design: Lisa Bachar
Editing: Cathy Christiansen, Carol Faino and Susan Larson

Front cover photos: ©Steve Murray/Picturesque (top);
©Jeff Sarpa/Stockfood America (bottom)
Back cover photo: ©Comstock Images/Alamy (bottom left)

3D Press, Inc.
2969 Baseline Road
Boulder, CO 80303
303-623-4484 (phone) / 303-623-4494 (fax)
info@3dpress.net (email)

888-456-3607 (order toll-free)
www.3dpress.net

The Bed & Breakfast Cookbook Series was originated by Carol Faino and Doreen Hazledine of Peppermint Press in Denver, CO in 1999.

Disclaimer and Limits of Liability

Recipes and descriptions of the bed and breakfast inns featured in this book are based on information supplied to us from sources believed to be reliable. While the authors and publisher have used their best efforts to insure the accuracy of all information at press time, the passage of time will always bring about change. Therefore, 3D Press, Inc. does not guarantee the accuracy or completeness of any information and is not responsible for any errors or omissions, or the results obtained from use of such information. The recipes chosen for inclusion are favorites of the inns and are not claimed to be original. Although the authors did not personally visit each inn, each recipe was home-kitchen tested, taste-tested and edited for clarity. This book is sold as is, without warranty of any kind, either expressed or implied. Neither the authors nor 3D Press, Inc. nor its distributors shall be liable to the purchaser or any other person or entity with respect to any liability, loss, or damage caused or alleged to be caused directly or indirectly by this book.

Introduction

If I could only taste my way through North Carolina, the experience itself would be a delight for the palette, but taking just one recipe from each of the distinct areas of our state through the Bed & Breakfast inns is more than one person should have access to in a lifetime.

Welcome to the *North Carolina Bed & Breakfast Cookbook*, featuring 120 delicious recipes from 62 members of the North Carolina Bed & Breakfast and Inns association. This book proves beyond a shadow of a doubt that North Carolina has some of the best cooks in our wonderful country.

From the Mountains to the Sea ... North Carolina is the place to be. Each of our participating inns has given you some of their best loved (and taste tested) recipes. Some are old family favorites, others are the result of years of experimentation or the requests of special guests.

Please bring a hearty appetite, eyes to see the beauty of the presentation of a great dish, a bowl of laughter, a platter of joy and most of all a comfortable chair to sit with friends and share these treasures from the kitchens of North Carolina's inspected B&B's and Country Inns.

The best way to test each of these wonderful dishes is to visit each of our inns. You can meet each inn online at www.ncbbi.org. Our true Southern hospitality abounds at each of our inns. Have a mountain top experience all the way to a seaside respite ... we welcome you to the wonderful world of North Carolina.

Happy Cooking!

Twyla Sickmiller
President
North Carolina Bed & Breakfast and Inns

Acknowledgements

Creating a book is a project involving many people. We owe a great deal of gratitude to the following friends, family members and business colleagues for their support, inspiration, enthusiasm, time and talents:

Cathy Christiansen, Carol Faino, Susan Larson, Twyla Sickmiller, president of the North Carolina Bed & Breakfast Association and a special thank you to the owners, innkeepers and chefs of the 62 North Carolina bed & breakfasts and country inns who generously and enthusiastically shared their favorite recipes and beautiful artwork.

Table of Contents

Breads, Biscuits, Scones & Muffins

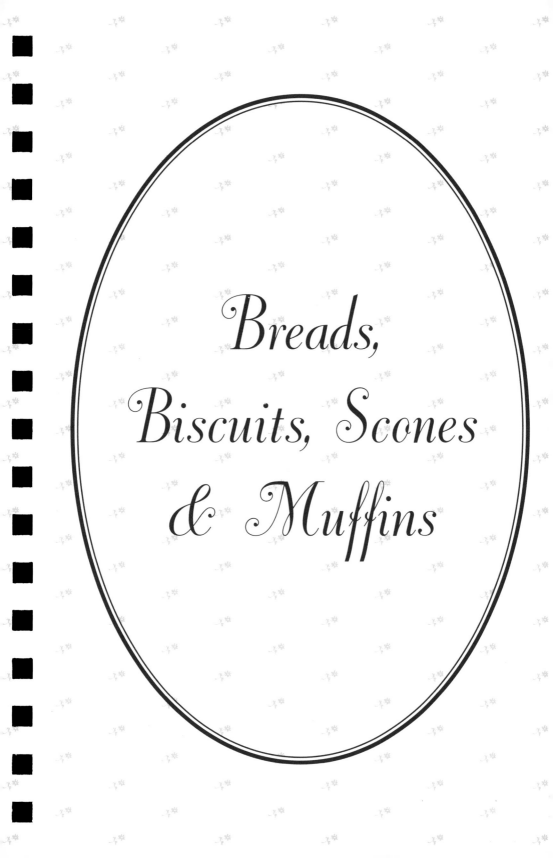

Breads, Biscuits, Scones & Muffins

Turn of the Century Victorian

The Turn of the Century Victorian Bed & Breakfast is the proud recipient of a 2001 Preservation North Carolina Award of Merit for the significant restoration of the house. A short stroll from the inviting front porch, guests can enjoy museums, restaurants, antiques and the charms of Salisbury's historic downtown.

Just a short distance from Salisbury, you can explore the North Carolina State Transportation Museum at Historic Spencer Shops, the High Point Furniture Market and Lowe's Motor Speedway.

INNKEEPERS:	Karen Windate
ADDRESS:	259 South Fulton Street
	Salisbury, North Carolina 28144
TELEPHONE:	(704) 642-1660; (800) 250-5349
E-MAIL:	info@turnofthecenturybb.com
WEBSITE:	www.turnofthecenturybb.com
ROOMS:	3 Rooms; 1 Suite; Private baths
CHILDREN:	Children age 12 and older welcome
ANIMALS:	Not allowed
HANDICAPPED:	Not handicapped accessible
DIETARY NEEDS:	Will accommodate guests' special dietary needs

Lemon Bread

Makes 1 Loaf

¾   stick butter, softened (or ½ stick butter plus 2 tablespoons shortening, softened)
1   cup sugar
1½   cups all-purpose flour
2   eggs
1   teaspoon baking powder
½   teaspoon salt
½   cup milk
Grated zest of 1 lemon

Glaze:
2   tablespoons sugar (or more for a sweeter glaze)
Juice of 1 lemon

Preheat oven to 325°F. Spray a 9x5-inch loaf pan with non-stick cooking spray or grease pan with shortening. Cream butter and sugar. Mix in flour, eggs, baking powder, salt, milk and lemon zest in order given. Pour batter into pan. Bake for 1 hour, or until a toothpick inserted in center comes out clean. Pour glaze over hot bread. Cool bread, then slice and serve.

For the glaze: Combine sugar and lemon juice; stir until sugar is dissolved.

Bed & Breakfast at Ponder Cove

The Bed & Breakfast at Ponder Cove not only allows your dog, but rolls out the red carpet for your pampered pet. The inn offers an off-leash play area, a doggy welcome basket and dog sitter and activity information. Deliberately off the beaten path, the inn is nestled in the Blue Ridge Mountains, which are part of the Great Smokies. This vacation paradise is tucked away in a 91-acre private cove, what the locals call a "holler."

Jack Jarvis, a Madison County native who has his own show on Home and Garden TV, designed the inn's gardens in a Japanese style.

INNKEEPERS:	Martha Abraham & Gary Rawlins
ADDRESS:	1067 Ponder Creek Road
	Mars Hill, North Carolina 28754
TELEPHONE:	(828) 689-7304; (866) 689-7304
E-MAIL:	martha@ponder.com
WEBSITE:	www.pondercove.com
ROOMS:	3 Suites; Private baths
CHILDREN:	Call ahead
ANIMALS:	Dogs welcome; Resident dogs
HANDICAPPED:	Not handicapped accessible
DIETARY NEEDS:	Will accommodate guests' special dietary needs

Nannie Bess' Banana Nut Bread

Makes 2 Loaves

"This recipe was handed down from my grandmother, Bessie Caroline Gatlin, born in 1904. She was a feisty Ozark woman known for her hospitality and good food. If you came to her home as a stranger, you left as a friend. I am sure this influence was behind my desire to be an innkeeper. How lucky I am to have the recipes she left behind. She had the right idea – grow it, cook it and spread goodwill through good food, family and friendship."~ Innkeeper, Bed & Breakfast at Ponder Cove

2	cups sugar
2	sticks butter, softened
½	cup vegetable oil, warmed
4	eggs, well beaten
1½	teaspoons vanilla extract
1½	cups chopped pecans
1½	cups raisins
3	cups all-purpose flour
2	teaspoons baking soda
½	teaspoon salt
6	very ripe bananas, mashed

Preheat oven to 350°F. Grease and flour 2 (9x5-inch) loaf pans. In a large bowl, with a mixer, cream sugar, butter and oil. Mix in eggs, vanilla, pecans and raisins. In a small bowl, combine flour, baking soda and salt. Add flour mixture to butter mixture and mix well. Add bananas and mix well.

Pour batter into pans. Bake for about 75 minutes, until bread begins to pull away from sides of pan and a toothpick inserted in center comes out clean (just make sure top is brown and let bread sit for a few minutes, it will continue to firm up as it cools).

Big Mill

The Big Mill Bed & Breakfast sits amid acres of farmland and forest in the quiet coastal plain of eastern North Carolina, about two hours from Raleigh and Norfolk, in a lush landscape where streams and rivers meander through cypress swamps and fertile farmland.

With over 200 acres of grounds, you can walk in the landscaped gardens, wander through woodlands or explore the original farm outbuildings. Shaded by stately, 89-year-old pecan trees planted by the owner's parents, the house has been in the innkeeper's family since 1920.

INNKEEPERS:	Chloe G. Tuttle
ADDRESS:	1607 Big Mill Road
	Williamston, North Carolina 27892
TELEPHONE:	(252) 792-8787
E-MAIL:	info@bigmill.com
WEBSITE:	www.bigmill.com
ROOMS:	2 Rooms; 2 Suites; Private baths
CHILDREN:	Children age 10 and older welcome
ANIMALS:	Not allowed; Resident outdoor cat
HANDICAPPED:	Not handicapped accessible
DIETARY NEEDS:	Will accommodate guests' special dietary needs

Sweet Potato Biscuits

Makes 70 Small Biscuits

1   cup canned sweet potatoes or yams, drained and mashed
1   cup packed light brown sugar
¼   cup water
2¼ cups packed Bisquick or biscuit mix

Preheat oven to 350°F. Combine sweet potatoes, brown sugar, water and Bisquick (mixture will be very sticky). On a floured surface, roll out dough ½- to ¾-inch thick (do not roll too thin or biscuits will be dry).

Cut biscuits with a 1½-inch biscuit cutter and place on a greased baking sheet, leaving some space between biscuits. Bake for 12-15 minutes (do not overbake – biscuits will be moist even when done). Remove biscuits to a wire rack and cool. Serve warm or at room temperature.

Serving suggestion: Split biscuits and stuff with salty, shaved Virginia or country ham (1 pound of ham will stuff 70 small biscuits).

Note: If making larger biscuits, increase baking time to 16-18 minutes.

Arrowhead Inn

The Arrowhead Inn is the only AAA Four Diamond and Select Registry bed & breakfast in the Triangle area of Raleigh, Durham and Chapel Hill. The inn has been featured in *Southern Living*, *House and Garden*, *Food & Wine*, *USA Today* and *Old House Journal*.

Awake to an abundant feast with such treats as puffed pancakes, blueberry French toast, fresh herb frittatas, yeast breads and baked fruits. Enjoy rich coffee and the sounds of Bach while engaged in quiet conversation.

INNKEEPERS:	Gloria & Phil Tebeo
ADDRESS:	106 Mason Road
	Durham, North Carolina 27712
TELEPHONE:	(800) 528-2207
E-MAIL:	info@arrowheadinn.com
WEBSITE:	www.arrowheadinn.com
ROOMS:	4 Rooms; 3 Suites; 2 Cottages; Private baths
CHILDREN:	Welcome
ANIMALS:	Not allowed
HANDICAPPED:	Handicapped accessible
DIETARY NEEDS:	Will accommodate guests' special dietary needs

Ginger Scones

Makes 12 Scones

3	cups all-purpose flour
1/3	cup sugar
1	tablespoon plus 1 teaspoon baking powder
1/4	teaspoon grated lemon zest
1	stick plus 3 tablespoons unsalted butter, chilled and diced
3/4	cup plus 2 tablespoons whipping cream or buttermilk
2/3	cup diced crystallized (candied) ginger

Preheat oven to 400°F. In a food processor, combine flour, sugar, baking powder and lemon zest. Add butter and pulse until mixture resembles a coarse meal (or cut in butter by hand with 2 knives). Transfer flour mixture to a large bowl and make a well in center. Add 3/4 cup of cream to well and stir with a fork just until flour mixture is moistened. Stir in ginger.

Transfer dough to a floured surface and knead gently until smooth, about 8 turns. Divide dough in half and pat each portion into a 3/4-inch-thick round. Cut each round into 6 wedges and place on a lightly buttered baking sheet, spacing scones 1-inch apart. Brush tops with the remaining 2 tablespoons of cream. Bake for about 18 minutes, until light brown. Cool completely, then store in an airtight container at room temperature.

Note: These scones can be baked 1 day ahead. Simply rewarm them in a preheated 350°F oven before serving.

Katherine's

While innkeeper Ineke Strongman was raised in the Netherlands, it may be her lifetime of traveling the world that has contributed most in creating the high style and rich detail found at Katherine's Bed & Breakfast. The inn reflects the many places she has visited in her years of exploring the globe, while her skill in decorating and her talent for historic restoration have combined to create this elegant and comfortable inn.

Each bedroom is a picture-perfect gem with private bath, down comforter, plush robes, fireplace and a special teddy bear to welcome you.

INNKEEPERS:	Ineke Strongman & Michael Pewther
ADDRESS:	43 Watauga Street
	Asheville, North Carolina 28801
TELEPHONE:	(828) 236-9494; (888) 325-3190
E-MAIL:	info@katherinesbandb.com
WEBSITE:	www.katherinesbandb.com
ROOMS:	5 Rooms; 1 Suite; Private baths
CHILDREN:	Children age 12 and older welcome
ANIMALS:	Not allowed; Resident cat
HANDICAPPED:	Not handicapped accessible
DIETARY NEEDS:	Will accommodate guests' special dietary needs

Cream Cheese Raisin Scones

Makes 18 Scones

*"This recipe is easy and fast. The scones are moist and need nothing on them. -
Innkeeper, Katherine's Bed & Breakfast*

1¾	cups plus 2 tablespoons all-purpose flour
3	tablespoons sugar
1	tablespoon baking powder
½	teaspoon salt
1	(8-ounce) package cream cheese, cut into small cubes
½	cup raisins
1	egg, beaten
½	cup milk
¼	cup whipping cream

Preheat oven to 350°F. Sift together flour, sugar, baking powder and salt
into a large bowl. Stir in cream cheese, leaving cream cheese in cubes. Add
raisins, 1 tablespoon of beaten egg, milk and cream; stir until combined,
leaving cream cheese in cubes to the extent possible.

Drop batter into mounds onto a baking sheet sprayed with non-stick
cooking spray, using 2 tablespoons of batter per scone and spacing mounds
1-inch apart. Brush tops of scones with remaining beaten egg and bake for
12-17 minutes, until golden brown.

The Inn at Bingham School

The circa 1796 Inn at Bingham School is located just west of Chapel Hill and the University of North Carolina, tucked away on ten acres under large pecan trees. Listed on the National Register of Historic Places, the inn once served as the homestead for the headmaster of the Bingham School, a preparatory school for young men awaiting entrance to UNC Chapel Hill.

Wake up to an elaborate breakfast served in the dining room or on the patio. Menus are seasonal and may include such specialties as pear almond waffles, baked German pancakes and huevos rancheros.

INNKEEPERS:	François & Christina Deprez
ADDRESS:	NC 54 at Mebane Oaks Road
	Chapel Hill, North Carolina 27514
TELEPHONE:	(919) 563-5583; (800) 566-5583
E-MAIL:	fdeprez@aol.com
WEBSITE:	www.chapel-hill-inn.com
ROOMS:	4 Rooms; 1 Cottage; Private baths
CHILDREN:	Welcome
ANIMALS:	Not allowed
HANDICAPPED:	Not handicapped accessible
DIETARY NEEDS:	Will accommodate guests' special dietary needs

Lemon Poppyseed Scones

Makes 12 Scones

3	cups all-purpose flour
1	cup plus 1 tablespoon sugar
2	tablespoons poppy seeds
1	tablespoon baking powder
2	teaspoons grated lemon zest
1	teaspoon salt
1	stick plus 2 tablespoons unsalted butter, diced
1	large egg
2	teaspoons lemon juice
½	cup plus ⅓ cup milk

Preheat oven to 375°F. In a food processor, combine flour, 1 cup of sugar, poppy seeds, baking powder, lemon zest and salt. Add butter and pulse to combine. Transfer flour mixture to a bowl. Whisk together egg and lemon juice; add to flour mixture. Stir in ½ cup of milk.

With your hands, gather dough into a ball. Divide dough in half. Flatten each half into a circle. Cut each circle into 6 wedges. Brush with remaining ⅓ cup of milk. Sprinkle with remaining 1 tablespoon of sugar. Bake until golden brown, about 25 minutes.

Thomas Walton Manor

Welcome to the Thomas Walton Manor, a bed & breakfast inn. Come in and savor the restful elegance of one of North Carolina's most gracious residences. Designed by John Weaver of New York City and modeled after plantations along the James River outside of Richmond, Virginia, this stately Georgian colonial was built in 1939.

As beautiful outside as inside, the garden area, designed by famed landscape designer Charles Gillette, is lush and replete with specimen camellias, a swimming pool, smokehouse retreat, herb garden and fish pond.

INNKEEPERS:	Ron Phillips, Larry Horne & Anne Moberg
ADDRESS:	400 West Church Street
	Laurinburg, North Carolina 28352
TELEPHONE:	(910) 276-0551
E-MAIL:	relax@thomaswaltonmanor.com
WEBSITE:	www.thomaswaltonmanor.com
ROOMS:	2 Rooms; 3 Suites; 1 Apartment; Private baths
CHILDREN:	Children age 14 and older welcome
ANIMALS:	Small dogs welcome in apartment
HANDICAPPED:	Not handicapped accessible
DIETARY NEEDS:	Will accommodate guests' special dietary needs

Applesauce Oatmeal Muffins

Makes 12 Muffins

"My family prefers golden raisins in these muffins, however, dried cranberries, currants or other dried fruit can be used." ~ Innkeeper, Thomas Walton Manor

1½	cups old-fashioned rolled oats
1¼	cups all-purpose flour
¾	teaspoon cinnamon
1	teaspoon baking powder
¾	teaspoon baking soda
1	cup unsweetened applesauce
½	cup skim milk
½	cup packed brown sugar
3	tablespoons vegetable oil
1	egg
¾	cup raisins

Topping:

½	cup old-fashioned rolled oats
2	tablespoons packed brown sugar
¼	teaspoon cinnamon
2	tablespoons butter, melted
¼	cup chopped pecans or other nuts (optional)

Preheat oven to 375°F. In a large bowl, combine oats, flour, cinnamon, baking powder and baking soda. In a medium bowl, combine applesauce, milk, brown sugar, oil, egg and raisins. Add applesauce mixture to oat mixture and stir just until oat mixture is moistened. Fill paper-lined or greased muffin cups almost full. Sprinkle topping over batter. Bake for 20-22 minutes, until deep brown.

For the topping: Combine topping ingredients.

Rosemary House

W elcome to the Rosemary House Bed & Breakfast, a gracious 1912 Colonial Revival house listed on the National Register of Historic Places. The inn is located in historic Pittsboro, near Chapel Hill and convenient to Raleigh and Durham.

A full breakfast is served in the dining room at the time of your choosing. Entrées may include vegetarian eggs Benedict, huevos rancheros, Belgian waffles or herb omelets accompanied by rosemary-roasted potatoes. For healthy eaters, oatmeal with apples, pecans and raisins is always offered.

INNKEEPERS:	Karen & Mac Pullen
ADDRESS:	76 West Street
	Pittsboro, North Carolina 27312
TELEPHONE:	(919) 542-5515; (888) 643-2017
E-MAIL:	karen@rosemary-bb.com
WEBSITE:	www.rosemary-bb.com
ROOMS:	5 Rooms; Private baths
CHILDREN:	Welcome
ANIMALS:	Not allowed
HANDICAPPED:	Not handicapped accessible
DIETARY NEEDS:	Will accommodate guests' special dietary needs

Apricot Pecan Muffins

Makes 12 Muffins

"These muffins are delicious and moist. They also freeze well." – Innkeeper, Rosemary House Bed & Breakfast

2	cups whole-wheat pastry flour (or white pastry flour)
½	cup sugar
1	teaspoon baking soda
¼	teaspoon salt
1	cup plain yogurt
¼	cup milk
¼	cup canola oil
1	large egg, beaten
2	tablespoons maple syrup
1	teaspoon vanilla extract
¾	cup chopped dried apricots
½	cup chopped pecans

Preheat oven to 350°F. Spray muffin cups with non-stick cooking spray. In a large bowl, mix flour, sugar, baking soda and salt. In a medium bowl, mix yogurt, milk, oil, egg, maple syrup and vanilla. Make a well in center of flour mixture. Add yogurt mixture to well and stir just to combine. Stir in apricots and pecans. Spoon batter into muffin cups. Bake for 20 minutes. Remove muffins from oven and cool for 5 minutes in pan, then remove from pan.

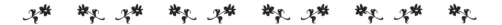

803 Elizabeth

The 803 Elizabeth Bed & Breakfast is nestled on five acres of woods and gardens. The inn is located in Matthews, a small town just 12 miles from downtown Charlotte that offers a wide range of unique dining and shopping opportunities.

803 Elizabeth has been designated as a Wildlife Habitat by the National Wildlife Federation. Something is in bloom every day of the year in the fabulous gardens at the inn. And each day, the garden changes with new blooms and colors.

INNKEEPERS:	Martha & Will Krauss
ADDRESS:	803 Elizabeth Lane
	Matthews, North Carolina 28105
TELEPHONE:	(704) 841-8900; (800) 327-4843
E-MAIL:	mwkrauss@carolina.rr.com
WEBSITE:	www.803elizabeth.com
ROOMS:	3 Rooms; Private baths
CHILDREN:	Children age 6 and older welcome
ANIMALS:	Not allowed
HANDICAPPED:	Not handicapped accessible
DIETARY NEEDS:	Will accommodate guests' special dietary needs

Low-Fat Applesauce Muffin Tops

Makes 12 Muffin Tops or 8 Regular Muffins

"This recipe is adapted from the book Innkeepers' Best Muffins *by Laura Zahn. The low fat content makes them heavier than usual muffins, but try them, you'll like them!" ~ Innkeeper, 803 Elizabeth Bed & Breakfast*

1¼   cups applesauce
1   teaspoon vanilla extract
1½   cups unbleached all-purpose flour
½   cup whole-wheat flour
½   cup plus 1 tablespoon sugar
1½   teaspoons baking powder
1   teaspoon baking soda
1   teaspoon cinnamon
½   cup chopped nuts
½   cup Craisins or dried cranberries
½   teaspoon nutmeg

Preheat oven to 350°F. In a large bowl, combine applesauce and vanilla. In a medium bowl, combine all-purpose and whole-wheat flours, ½ cup of sugar, baking powder, baking soda and cinnamon. Add flour mixture to applesauce mixture and stir just to combine (do not overmix). Stir in nuts and Craisins.

Spoon batter (or use an ice cream scoop) into greased or paper-lined muffin top or regular muffin cups. Combine nutmeg and remaining 1 tablespoon of sugar; sprinkle about ¼ teaspoon of nutmeg mixture over batter in each muffin cup. Bake for 20-25 minutes.

Meadows Inn

B uilt in 1980 as weekend lodging for visitors coming to see the Tryon Palace, the Meadows Inn has grown to offer year-round accommodations. Nestled peacefully in the heart of the downtown historic district, the inn is within walking distance of the Tryon Palace and Garden, shops, excellent restaurants and the birthplace of Pepsi.

The Tryon Palace was built between 1767 and 1770 as the first permanent capitol of the colony of North Carolina and a home for the royal governor and his family.

INNKEEPERS:	John & Betty Foy
ADDRESS:	212 Pollock Street
	New Bern, North Carolina 28560
TELEPHONE:	(252) 634-1776; (877) 551-1776
E-MAIL:	meadowsinnbnb@earthlink.net
WEBSITE:	www.meadowsinn-nc.com
ROOMS:	6 Rooms; 1 Suite; Private baths
CHILDREN:	Welcome
ANIMALS:	Not allowed
HANDICAPPED:	Not handicapped accessible
DIETARY NEEDS:	Will accommodate guests' special dietary needs

Morning Glory Muffins

Makes 18 Muffins

2	cups all-purpose flour
1	cup sugar
2	teaspoons baking soda
2	teaspoons cinnamon
½	teaspoon salt
2	cups grated carrots (about 3 medium carrots)
1	apple, peeled and grated
½	cup raisins
½	cup shredded coconut
½	cup chopped pecans
3	eggs, lightly beaten
1	cup vegetable oil
2	teaspoons vanilla extract

Preheat oven to 350°F. Sift together flour, sugar, baking soda, cinnamon and salt into a large bowl. Stir in carrots, apple, raisins, coconut and pecans. In a medium bowl, combine eggs, oil and vanilla; add to flour mixture and stir just until moist and smooth. Pour batter into greased or paper-lined muffin cups. Bake for 30-35 minutes, until firm and puffed.

Inn on Main Street

Western North Carolina is a mecca for outdoor enthusiasts. There are thousands of miles of trophy trout streams joining rivers where whitewater rafters and kayakers can take in the mountain beauty up close. Where highland valleys meet climbing hills, some of the most beautiful golf courses in the nation challenge all skill levels and inn guests get a discount at Reems Creek Golf Club, which is one of the best.

An hour west of the inn, Great Smoky Mountains National Park contains more plant and animal species than any other National Park in America.

INNKEEPERS:	Dan & Nancy Ward
ADDRESS:	88 South Main Street
	Weaverville, North Carolina 28787
TELEPHONE:	(828) 645-4935; (877) 873-6074
E-MAIL:	relax@innonmain.com
WEBSITE:	www.innonmain.com
ROOMS:	7 Rooms; Private baths
CHILDREN:	Children age 12 and older welcome
ANIMALS:	Not allowed; Resident outdoor dog
HANDICAPPED:	Not handicapped accessible
DIETARY NEEDS:	Will accommodate guests' special dietary needs

Sweet Potato Muffins

Makes 8 to 12 Muffins

½   cup vegetable oil
1   cup packed brown sugar
1   teaspoon baking soda
1   teaspoon vanilla extract
3   tablespoons molasses
¼   teaspoon ground cloves
¼   teaspoon nutmeg
½   teaspoon ground ginger
1   large sweet potato, peeled and grated
1   egg
1   cup buttermilk
2½   cups all-purpose flour

Preheat oven to 350°F. In a large bowl, add and mix ingredients in order given, 1 at a time (batter should be thicker than pancake batter, but thinner than cookie dough). Fill greased or paper-lined muffin cups with batter to rim of cups. Bake for about 20 minutes, until tops are slightly browned.

Herren House

The Herren House is an 1897 boarding house located near Asheville in the heart of downtown Waynesville, "the gateway to the Smokies." The inn is the perfect spot for a getaway to the beautiful Cold Mountains. In less than a mile, the countryside begins to rise into some of the most majestic scenery in the eastern United States.

World-class art and cultural events keep things lively in town throughout the seasons, and the Great Smoky Mountains and the Blue Ridge Parkway are only a few minutes drive from the inn.

INNKEEPERS:	Jerry & Tom Halsey
ADDRESS:	94 East Street
	Waynesville, North Carolina 28786
TELEPHONE:	(828) 452-7837; (800) 284-1932
E-MAIL:	herren@brinet.com
WEBSITE:	www.herrenhouse.com
ROOMS:	6 Rooms; Private baths
CHILDREN:	Children age 12 and older welcome
ANIMALS:	Not allowed; Resident dog
HANDICAPPED:	Handicapped accessible
DIETARY NEEDS:	Will accommodate guests' special dietary needs

Bacon Chive Muffins

Makes 12 Muffins

1½	cups all-purpose flour
2	teaspoons baking powder
½	teaspoon salt
2	teaspoons sugar
1	cup grated Swiss or cheddar cheese
¼	cup finely chopped chives or green onions
6	slices bacon, cooked crisp, drained and crumbled
1	egg
¾	cup milk or half & half
1	tablespoon Dijon mustard
¼	cup canola or vegetable oil

Preheat oven to 400°F. Sift together flour, baking powder and salt into a large bowl. Stir in sugar, cheese and chives. Add bacon, egg, milk, mustard and oil; mix just until blended.

Pour batter into muffin cups sprayed with non-stick cooking spray. Bake for 15-20 minutes, until golden brown. Remove muffins from oven and cool for 2 minutes in pan, then remove muffins from pan. Serve warm.

Coffee Cakes & Granola

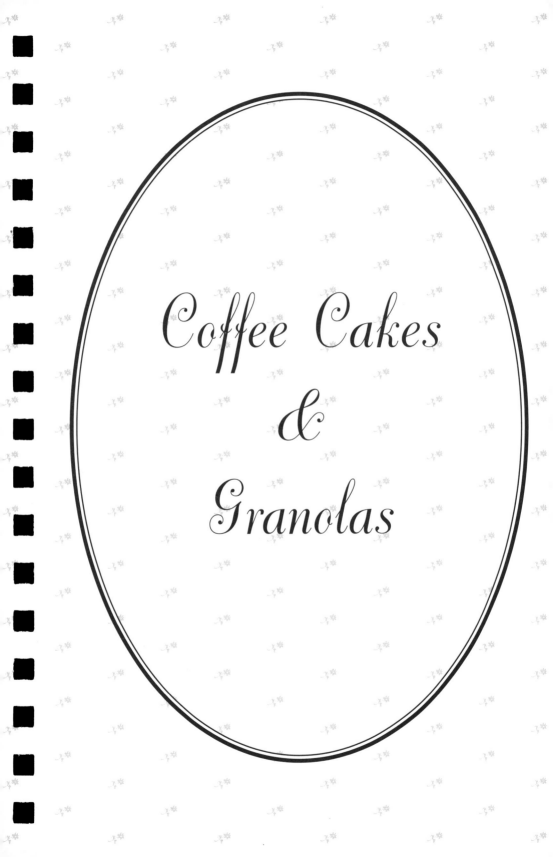

Coffee Cakes

&

Granolas

Barrister's

Enjoy Southern hospitality and a family atmosphere in one of Roxboro's most historic structures. Barrister's Bed & Breakfast is conveniently located near Raleigh-Durham and is two blocks from uptown Roxboro and the Person County History Museum.

Built in 1921, this Georgian Revival home features architectural details including a grand staircase, handmade columns and beveled glass doors and mahogany beams in the foyer. Handpainted art is found on the dining room ceiling mural, family crest panels and living room cornice.

INNKEEPERS:	**Cindy & Alan Hicks**
ADDRESS:	**400 North Main Street**
	Roxboro, North Carolina 27573
TELEPHONE:	**(336) 597-2848**
E-MAIL:	**barristersbedbreakfast@yahoo.com**
WEBSITE:	**www.barristersbedbreakfast.com**
ROOMS:	**3 Rooms; Private baths**
CHILDREN:	**Children age 10 and older welcome**
ANIMALS:	**Not allowed**
HANDICAPPED:	**Not handicapped accessible**
DIETARY NEEDS:	**Will accommodate guests' special dietary needs**

Almond Skillet Coffee Cake

Makes 10 Servings

1½   cups sugar plus extra, for topping
1   stick butter, melted
½   stick margarine, melted
2   eggs
1½   cups all-purpose flour
Pinch of salt
1   teaspoon almond extract
¼   cup slivered almonds

Preheat oven to 350°F. In a bowl, combine 1½ cups of sugar, butter and margarine; stir to combine. Beat in eggs, 1 at a time. Add flour, salt and almond extract; mix well.

Line an 8-inch cast-iron skillet with aluminum foil. Pour batter into skillet. Sprinkle batter with slivered almonds, then with sugar. Bake for 35 minutes. Remove cake from skillet, slice and serve.

The Boxley

The Boxley Bed & Breakfast Inn is set on over an acre of landscaped grounds in downtown Madison, just 22 miles north of Greensboro. Within a 30-minute drive, you can find the heart of High Point and the High Point Furniture Market, downtown Winston-Salem and Old Salem. For the adventurous, Hanging Rock State Park is just 20 minutes away.

Come and enjoy a 19th century setting and the peacefulness and serenity of the inn's yard and gardens. Relax and listen to the birds, smell the flowers and watch the beautiful sunset from the inn.

INNKEEPERS:	JoAnn & Monte McIntosh
ADDRESS:	117 East Hunter Street
	Madison, North Carolina 27025
TELEPHONE:	(336) 427-0453; (800) 429-3516
E-MAIL:	info@greensboro-inn.com
WEBSITE:	www.boxleybedandbreakfast.com
ROOMS:	3 Rooms; 1 Cottage; Private baths
CHILDREN:	Welcome
ANIMALS:	Not allowed; Resident dog
HANDICAPPED:	Not handicapped accessible
DIETARY NEEDS:	Will accommodate guests' special dietary needs

Cream Cheese Coffee Cake

Makes 24 Squares

"I received this recipe from a dear friend in Kentucky." ~ Innkeeper, The Boxley Bed & Breakfast Inn

2   (8-ounce) packages crescent rolls
1   (8-ounce) package cream cheese, softened
1   cup sugar
1   teaspoon vanilla extract
1   large egg yolk

Glaze:
1   cup powdered sugar
2   tablespoons milk

Preheat oven to 350°F. Unroll 1 package of crescent rolls and spread in a 9x13-inch baking pan; seal perforations. Combine cream cheese, sugar, vanilla and egg yolk; spread on top of rolls in pan. Unroll second package of rolls and spread on top of cream cheese mixture; seal perforations. Bake for 28 minutes, or until lightly browned. Cool for 30 minutes, then spread with glaze. Serve warm, or cover and refrigerate overnight and serve cold.

For the glaze: Mix powdered sugar and milk until smooth and thick.

Flint Street Inns

The Flint Street Inns occupy two lovely, early 20th century homes on an acre of landscaped grounds featuring stately old trees, flower gardens and fish ponds. The inn is located in the midst of the Montford Historic District, Asheville's oldest neighborhood, and is within comfortable walking distance of the historic Art Deco downtown area.

Downtown Asheville is wonderful to explore with its excellent restaurants, sidewalk cafes, bookstores, antique shops and arts and craft galleries.

INNKEEPERS:	Rick, Lynne & Marion Vogel
ADDRESS:	116 Flint Street
	Asheville, North Carolina 28801
TELEPHONE:	(828) 253-6723; (800) 234-8172
E-MAIL:	flintstreetinns@cs.com
WEBSITE:	www.flintstreetinns.com
ROOMS:	8 Rooms; Private baths
CHILDREN:	Children age 14 and older welcome
ANIMALS:	Not allowed
HANDICAPPED:	Not handicapped accessible
DIETARY NEEDS:	Will accommodate guests' special dietary needs

Apple Sour Cream Coffee Cake

Makes 1 Cake

½	cup chopped nuts
2	teaspoons cinnamon
1½	cups sugar, divided
1	stick butter
2	eggs
1	teaspoon vanilla extract
2	cups all-purpose flour
1	teaspoon baking powder
1	teaspoon baking soda
½	teaspoon salt
1	cup sour cream
1	medium apple, peeled, cored and thinly sliced

Preheat oven to 350°F. Grease well and flour a 9x5-inch loaf pan. In a small bowl, combine nuts, cinnamon and ½ cup of sugar. In a large bowl, with a mixer at high speed, cream butter and remaining 1 cup of sugar until light and fluffy. Add eggs, 1 at a time, beating well after each addition. Mix in vanilla. Add flour, baking powder, baking soda and salt; beat well. Mix in sour cream.

Spread ½ of batter in pan. Top with apples, then with ½ of nut mixture. Add remaining batter, then top with remaining nut mixture. Bake for 40 minutes, or until a toothpick inserted in center comes out clean. Remove cake from oven and cool in pan on a wire rack for 30 minutes. Loosen edges of cake and remove from pan. Cool cake completely on a wire rack, then slice and serve.

Note: The whole, unsliced cake freezes well.

The White Doe Inn

The White Doe Inn harkens back to an era when guests were pampered, and the innkeepers make every effort to recapture that era of traveler comfort and camaraderie. Guest rooms and suites are distinctively decorated with family heirlooms and turn-of-the-century antiques. Rooms feature bedside gas-log fireplaces and several offer spa tubs for two.

Guests returning to the inn after a day of fun-filled adventure on the Outer Banks will find wonderful and delightful homemade desserts, a selection of Harney & Sons famous teas and delicious Green Mountain Roasted Coffee.

INNKEEPERS:	Bebe & Bob Woody
ADDRESS:	319 Sir Walter Raleigh Street
	Manteo, North Carolina 27954
TELEPHONE:	(252) 473-9851; (800) 473-6091
E-MAIL:	whitedoe@whitedoeinn.com
WEBSITE:	www.whitedoeinn.com
ROOMS:	8 Rooms; Private baths
CHILDREN:	Children age 12 and older welcome
ANIMALS:	Not allowed; Resident dog
HANDICAPPED:	Not handicapped accessible
DIETARY NEEDS:	Will accommodate guests' special dietary needs

Raspberry Cream Cheese Coffee Cake

Makes 1 Cake

"This is our signature coffee cake." ~ Innkeeper, The White Doe Inn Bed & Breakfast

2 ¼   cups all-purpose flour
1   cup sugar, divided
1½   sticks butter
½   teaspoon baking powder
½   teaspoon baking soda
1   teaspoon almond extract
¾   cup sour cream
3   eggs, divided
1   (8-ounce) package cream cheese, softened
⅔   cup seedless raspberry preserves
½   cup sliced almonds

Preheat oven to 350°F. Grease and flour a 10-inch springform pan. In a large bowl, combine flour and ¾ cup of sugar. Cut in butter with a pastry blender or two knives until mixture is crumbly. Remove 1 cup of flour mixture and set aside for topping. Add baking powder, baking soda, almond extract, sour cream and 1 egg to flour mixture in the large bowl; mix well and spread mixture over bottom and 2 inches up sides of pan.

Combine cream cheese, remaining ¼ cup of sugar and remaining 2 eggs; mix well and spoon over crust. Carefully spoon raspberry preserves over cream cheese mixture. Combine reserved 1 cup of flour mixture and almonds; sprinkle over preserves. Bake for 45-55 minutes. Cool for 15 minutes in pan, then remove sides of pan and cool cake completely.

Pecan Tree Inn

L ocated in the heart of the Beaufort Historic District and just steps from the scenic yacht harbor, the Pecan Tree Inn is known as the place to stay when visiting the Carolina coast and the southern Outer Banks.

The white sandy beaches of Cape Lookout, Shackleford Banks and Atlantic Beach are nearby. Historic Beaufort has over 100 beautifully restored 18th and 19th century homes and a growing collection of fine restaurants and shops. The deep-water harbor is a favorite port of call for yachts from around the world. You might say that Beaufort is Nantucket with a Southern drawl.

INNKEEPERS:	Dave & Allison DuBuisson
ADDRESS:	116 Queen Street
	Beaufort, North Carolina 28516
TELEPHONE:	(252) 728-6733; (800) 728-7871
E-MAIL:	innkeeper@pecantree.com
WEBSITE:	www.pecantree.com
ROOMS:	7 Rooms; Private baths
CHILDREN:	Children age 10 and older welcome
ANIMALS:	Not allowed
HANDICAPPED:	Not handicapped accessible
DIETARY NEEDS:	Will accommodate guests' special dietary needs

Nutmeg Coffee Cake

Makes 12 to 15 Servings

"This coffee cake is light in texture and absolutely delicious. The delicate flavor of nutmeg is a nice change from cinnamon for breakfast. Best yet, it can be prepared a day ahead and baked in the morning." ~ Innkeeper, Pecan Tree Inn

Cake:
2¼	cups all-purpose flour
½	cup white sugar
½	cup packed brown sugar
2	teaspoons baking powder
1	teaspoon baking soda
½	teaspoon salt
1	cup buttermilk
1	stick plus 3 tablespoons butter, softened
2	large eggs

Topping:
½	cup packed brown sugar
½	cup chopped nuts
½	teaspoon nutmeg

For the cake: Preheat oven to 350°F. Grease and flour a 9x13-inch baking pan. In a large bowl, combine all cake ingredients and beat with a mixer at low speed until combined, then beat at medium speed for about 2 minutes. Pour batter into pan. Sprinkle topping over batter (if desired, cover and refrigerate overnight). Bake for 30-35 minutes, or until a toothpick inserted in center comes out clean. Cool for at least 15-20 minutes before slicing and serving.

For the topping: Combine topping ingredients.

Bed & Breakfast at Laurel Ridge

Laurel Ridge is conveniently located between the Triangle (Chapel Hill and Raleigh-Durham) and the Triad (Winston-Salem, Greensboro and High Point). With pottery shopping, furniture hunting, antique browsing, visiting the zoo or just relaxing, a rewarding stay awaits.

Breakfasts change with the seasons, using the freshest ingredients possible. Innkeeper David Simmons is an accomplished chef by trade and brings his expertise to the breakfast table with such treats as cheddar and chili soufflé, pumpkin basil pancakes, eggs Benedict and freshly baked pastries.

INNKEEPERS:	David Simmons
ADDRESS:	3188 Silver City Snow Camp Road
	Silver City, North Carolina 27344
TELEPHONE:	(919) 742-6049; (800) 742-6049
E-MAIL:	davids@pinehurst.net
WEBSITE:	www.laurel-ridge.com
ROOMS:	2 Rooms; 1 Suite; 1 Cottage; Private baths
CHILDREN:	Children age 10 and older welcome
ANIMALS:	Not allowed; Resident cats
HANDICAPPED:	Handicapped accessible
DIETARY NEEDS:	Will accommodate guests' special dietary needs

Lemon Rosemary Crumb Cake

Makes 8 Servings

1¼	cups all-purpose flour
⅔	cup sugar
⅛	teaspoon salt
½	stick butter, cut into small pieces
¾	teaspoon chopped fresh rosemary
½	teaspoon baking powder
¼	teaspoon baking soda
⅓	cup buttermilk
2	tablespoons lemon juice
1	egg
2	teaspoons grated lemon zest
¾	teaspoon water

Preheat oven to 350°F. Spray an 8x8-inch baking pan with non-stick cooking spray. In a bowl, combine flour, sugar and salt. Cut in butter until mixture is the consistency of cornmeal. Remove ½ cup of flour mixture and set aside.

Add rosemary, baking powder and baking soda to flour mixture in bowl; stir to combine. Add buttermilk, lemon juice and egg; beat with a mixer on medium-low speed until blended. Spoon batter into baking pan.

Add lemon zest and water to reserved ½ cup of flour mixture; sprinkle over batter. Bake for 30 minutes, or until a toothpick inserted in center comes out clean.

Barrister's

The dining room at Barrister's Bed & Breakfast features a hand-painted mural on the ceiling along with a set of antique furniture, showcasing the hand-carved dining room table that belonged to the grandparents of innkeeper Cindy Hicks.

The guest sitting room is upstairs, just outside the three guest rooms, and offers the chance to relax, chat with fellow guests or catch up on a good book. The game room features a billiards table, board games, cards and a mini-fridge.

INNKEEPERS:	Cindy & Alan Hicks
ADDRESS:	400 North Main Street
	Roxboro, North Carolina 27573
TELEPHONE:	(336) 597-2848
E-MAIL:	barristersbedbreakfast@yahoo.com
WEBSITE:	www.barristersbedbreakfast.com
ROOMS:	3 Rooms; Private baths
CHILDREN:	Children age 10 and older welcome
ANIMALS:	Not allowed
HANDICAPPED:	Not handicapped accessible
DIETARY NEEDS:	Will accommodate guests' special dietary needs

Orange Breakfast Ring

Makes 10 Servings

5⅓ tablespoons butter, melted
1   cup sugar
3   tablespoons grated orange zest
2   (12-ounce) cans refrigerated buttermilk biscuits
1   (3-ounce) package cream cheese, softened
½   cup sifted powdered sugar
2   tablespoons orange juice

Preheat oven to 350°F. Combine melted butter, sugar and orange zest. Separate biscuits and dip each in butter mixture. Stand biscuits on edge in a 9-inch Bundt pan. Bake for 30 minutes, or until golden brown. Invert rolls onto a plate.

Combine cream cheese and powdered sugar until smooth. Add orange juice and stir well. Drizzle over hot rolls. Serve warm.

Pecan Tree Inn

The Pecan Tree Inn sits on a lot deeded to the Franklin Masonic Lodge in 1866 by Rebecca Piggott. It was converted to a private residence in 1900 and became an inn in 1992.

"One Beaufort hostelry of special note is the Pecan Tree Inn, housed in the elegant and historic Franklin Lodge. It is surely one of the most beautifully decorated and landscaped lodgings you will ever find. For my money, this is the spot for shoreside accommodations in Beaufort. The innkeepers are simply wonderful." ~ *Cruising Guide to Coastal North Carolina*

INNKEEPERS:	Dave & Allison DuBuisson
ADDRESS:	116 Queen Street
	Beaufort, North Carolina 28516
TELEPHONE:	(252) 728-6733; (800) 728-7871
E-MAIL:	innkeeper@pecantree.com
WEBSITE:	www.pecantree.com
ROOMS:	7 Rooms; Private baths
CHILDREN:	Children age 10 and older welcome
ANIMALS:	Not allowed
HANDICAPPED:	Not handicapped accessible
DIETARY NEEDS:	Will accommodate guests' special dietary needs

Pecan Tree Inn Granola

Makes 7 Cups

"This makes a fluffy, not sticky granola that can be tailored to your taste. Use your favorite dried fruits, nuts and grains to total seven cups of dry ingredients. Our favorite version contains golden raisins and pecans." ~ Innkeeper, Pecan Tree Inn

4	cups old-fashioned rolled oats
1	cup rolled wheat flakes
½	cup wheat germ
1	cup chopped nuts
¼	cup sesame seeds
¼	cup sunflower seeds
⅛	teaspoon salt
¼	cup plus 2 tablespoons vegetable oil
3	tablespoons water
¼	cup plus 2 tablespoons honey, warmed slightly (aids mixing)
¼	teaspoon vanilla extract
1	cup dried fruit, such as golden raisins, cherries, cranberries, etc.

Preheat oven to 225°F. In a very large bowl, combine oats, wheat flakes, wheat germ, nuts, sesame seeds, sunflower seeds and salt. In a small bowl, combine oil, water, honey and vanilla. Pour oil mixture over oat mixture and mix thoroughly. Spread granola on 2 rimmed baking sheets. Bake for 60 minutes, stirring every 10-15 minutes. Pour granola into a large bowl. Mix in dried fruit and cool. Store in an airtight container.

The White Doe Inn

As one of the most photographed historic homes on Roanoke Island, the White Doe Inn has been welcoming guests since the turn-of-the-century. Today, once again, guests can come to experience gracious hospitality in this lovely old home.

In the heart of the Outer Banks, just minutes from the Atlantic Ocean and its beautiful beaches, Roanoke Island is surrounded by the tranquil waters of the Croatan and Pamlico Sounds. Here, you will find the lovely waterfront village of Manteo and the White Doe Inn.

INNKEEPERS:	Bebe & Bob Woody
ADDRESS:	319 Sir Walter Raleigh Street
	Manteo, North Carolina 27954
TELEPHONE:	(252) 473-9851; (800) 473-6091
E-MAIL:	whitedoe@whitedoeinn.com
WEBSITE:	www.whitedoeinn.com
ROOMS:	8 Rooms; Private baths
CHILDREN:	Children age 12 and older welcome
ANIMALS:	Not allowed; Resident dog
HANDICAPPED:	Not handicapped accessible
DIETARY NEEDS:	Will accommodate guests' special dietary needs

Maple Crunch Cereal

Makes 6 to 7 Cups

"Served with just milk or topped with fresh fruit and yogurt, this cereal is packed full of all the right stuff for a busy day of sightseeing." ~ Innkeeper, The White Doe Inn Bed & Breakfast

2	cups old-fashioned rolled oats
4 ¼	cups wheat flakes cereal
1	tablespoon sesame seeds
⅓	cup sunflower seeds
⅓	cup shredded unsweetened coconut
1	cup chopped walnuts
⅓	cup maple syrup
⅓	cup sunflower oil

Preheat oven to 250°F. In a large bowl, combine oats, wheat flakes, sesame seeds, sunflower seeds, coconut and walnuts. Heat maple syrup and sunflower oil in a small saucepan over low heat until thinned and combined; pour over oats mixture and mix well. Spread mixture on a large, rimmed baking sheet. Bake for 1 hour, turning frequently, until toasted all over. Cool and store in a large, airtight container.

Pancakes, Fritters & Waffles

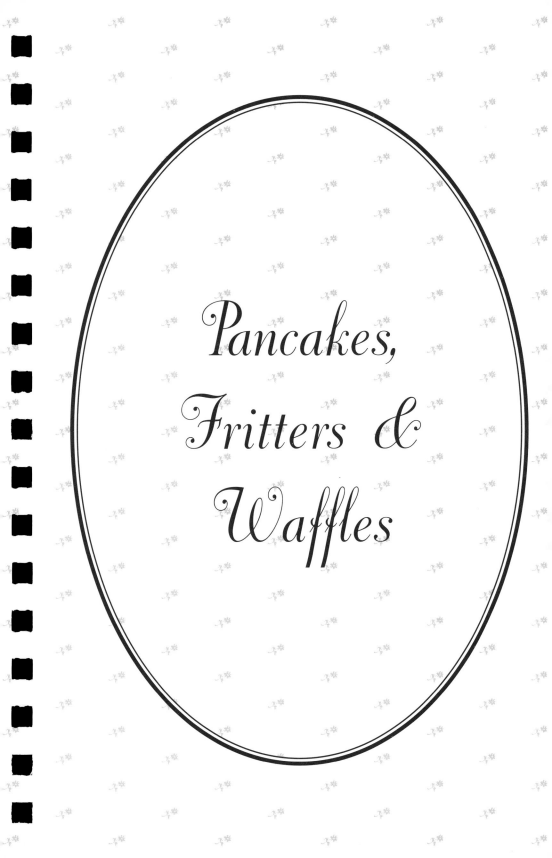

Pancakes, Fritters & Waffles

Colby House

The circa 1924, AAA Three Diamond Colby House offers discriminating travelers an elegant retreat a bygone era. It offers all the comforts of modern living and none of the pressures. Located in the heart of Asheville, in the Montford Historic District, the inn is within one mile of downtown shopping, dining and entertainment.

The Celebration Cottage boasts a cozy atmosphere with a parlor featuring a fireplace, kitchen and whirlpool tub with separate shower. A patio in the shady English garden, just outside the door, is enhanced by a Koi fish pond.

INNKEEPERS:	Peter & Bonnie Marsh
ADDRESS:	230 Pearson Drive
	Asheville, North Carolina 28801
TELEPHONE:	(828) 253-5644; (800) 982-2118
E-MAIL:	colbyhouse@cs.com
WEBSITE:	www.colbyhouse.com
ROOMS:	4 Rooms; 1 Cottage; Private baths
CHILDREN:	Call ahead
ANIMALS:	Not allowed
HANDICAPPED:	Not handicapped accessible
DIETARY NEEDS:	Will accommodate guests' special dietary needs

Lemon Ricotta Pancakes

Makes 6 to 8 Pancakes

3   eggs, separated
¼   cup all-purpose flour
½   cup vegetable oil
¾   cup ricotta cheese
2   tablespoons sugar
¼   teaspoon salt
1   tablespoon grated lemon zest
Fresh berries, for serving
Jam, for serving

In a large bowl, beat egg yolks, flour, oil, ricotta, sugar, salt and lemon zest. In a medium bowl, beat egg whites to soft peaks, then gently fold into egg yolk mixture. Pour batter onto a hot, greased griddle or skillet, using about 3 tablespoons of batter (just less than a ¼ cup) per pancake. Cook for about 2 minutes, then turn and cook for 1 minute more, until golden brown on each side. Serve with berries and jam.

Maxwell House

Come stay in the Maxwell House, a 1901 Victorian home located in the foothills of the Blue Ridge Mountains and the Wine Country. The Maxwell House is located in Mt. Airy, home to Andy Griffith and Donna Fargo. Mayberry Days are celebrated in September. In October, come for the Autumn Leaves Festival and celebrate the spectacular fall colors.

When staying at the Maxwell House, you will not leave the table hungry or be in want of a thing until dinner time. Breakfast includes scones, muffins, quiches, stratas and fresh seasonal fruit and juices.

INNKEEPERS:	Twyla & Roger Sickmiller
ADDRESS:	618 North Main Street
	Mt. Airy, North Carolina 27030
TELEPHONE:	(336) 786-2174; (877) 786-2174
E-MAIL:	maxwellhousebb@hotmail.com
WEBSITE:	www.bbonline.com/nc/maxwellhouse
ROOMS:	4 Rooms; Private baths
CHILDREN:	Children age 12 and older welcome
ANIMALS:	Not allowed
HANDICAPPED:	Handicapped accessible; 1 room
DIETARY NEEDS:	Will accommodate guests' special dietary needs

Authentic German Pancakes with Snow on the Mountain

Makes 6 to 8 Servings

"This is the one recipe everyone asks for." ~ Innkeeper, Maxwell House Bed & Breakfast

¾ cup self-rising flour
6 eggs
1 cup milk
¼ teaspoon salt
Lemon juice
4 large apples
½ stick butter
3 tablespoons cinnamon
1 cup packed brown sugar
Powdered sugar, for garnish
Maple syrup, for serving (optional)

Preheat oven to 350°F. In a large bowl, combine flour, eggs, milk and salt; mix until smooth. Peel and thinly slice apples into bowl. Sprinkle with lemon juice (lemon juice keeps apples from turning brown).

Melt butter in 9x13-inch glass baking dish in oven. Drain apples and arrange on top of butter in dish. Bake for 5 minutes, then remove from oven and slowly pour batter over apples. Combine cinnamon and brown sugar; sprinkle over batter. Bake for 30 minutes.

Slice and sprinkle with powdered sugar ("snow on the mountain"). Serve with warm maple syrup, if desired (the pancake is rich enough that it really doesn't need syrup).

The Verandas

The Verandas is an elegant 8,500-square-foot Victorian Italianate mansion located in the beautiful Wilmington Historic District. Only two blocks from the Cape Fear River and the Riverwalk, the inn is within walking distance of upscale shops and fine restaurants. It is a 15-minute drive to Wrightsville Beach, one of North Carolina's finest beaches!

Guests are encouraged to socialize in one of the two luxurious parlors, daydream on one of four verandas, meet on the garden terrace or just linger on the screened-in porch.

INNKEEPERS:	Dennis Madsen & Charles Pennington
ADDRESS:	202 Nun Street
	Wilmington, North Carolina 28401
TELEPHONE:	(910) 251-2212
E-MAIL:	verandas4@aol.com
WEBSITE:	www.verandas.com
ROOMS:	8 Rooms; Private baths
CHILDREN:	Children age 12 and older welcome
ANIMALS:	Not allowed; Resident cat
HANDICAPPED:	Not handicapped accessible
DIETARY NEEDS:	Will accommodate guests' special dietary needs

Blueberry Sour Cream Pancakes

Makes 4 Servings

1⅓ cups all-purpose flour
1   teaspoon salt
1½   teaspoons baking soda
1   tablespoon sugar
¼   teaspoon freshly grated nutmeg
1   egg, beaten
1   cup sour cream
1   cup milk
1   cup fresh blueberries

Blueberry syrup:
1   cup fresh blueberries
½   cup sugar
¾   cup water

In a large bowl, thoroughly combine flour, salt, baking soda, sugar and nutmeg. In a medium bowl, combine egg, sour cream and milk; add to flour mixture, stirring just enough to combine ingredients. Add blueberries, gently stirring just enough to mix (but not crush) blueberries. Drop batter onto a hot, greased griddle. Cook pancakes until golden on each side. Top with blueberry syrup or other favorite syrup to serve.

For the blueberry syrup: Combine syrup ingredients in a small saucepan over medium heat. Bring to a boil. Crush berries with the back of a spoon. Lower heat and simmer for 2-3 minutes. Serve warm.

Herren House

Located in the heart of downtown Waynesville – "the gateway to the Smokies" – the Herren House Bed & Breakfast provides the perfect spot for a getaway to North Carolina's beautiful Cold Mountain. Only one block to downtown Waynesville and 30 minutes to Asheville and the Biltmore Estate, the inn is central to hiking, rafting and beautiful drives.

Guests who are fortunate enough to stay at the inn for Saturday dinner can sit back and enjoy an elegant, five-course, gourmet meal by candlelight in the dining room or in the gardens (weather permitting).

INNKEEPERS:	Jerry & Tom Halsey
ADDRESS:	94 East Street
	Waynesville, North Carolina 28786
TELEPHONE:	(828) 452-7837; (800) 284-1932
E-MAIL:	herren@brinet.com
WEBSITE:	www.herrenhouse.com
ROOMS:	6 Rooms; Private baths
CHILDREN:	Children age 12 and older welcome
ANIMALS:	Not allowed; Resident dog
HANDICAPPED:	Handicapped accessible
DIETARY NEEDS:	Will accommodate guests' special dietary needs

Corn & Sweet Pepper Pancakes

Makes 20 (3-inch) Pancakes

2	tablespoons olive oil
½	cup diced red bell pepper
½	cup sliced green onion
⅓	cup minced fresh parsley
1	tablespoon fresh lemon juice
1	teaspoon salt
1	teaspoon sugar
¾	teaspoon dried oregano
¾	teaspoon cumin
¼	teaspoon black pepper
3½	cups frozen corn, cooked according to package directions and drained (or drained canned corn)
½	cup heavy cream
3	eggs, separated
½	cup unbleached all-purpose flour
¼	teaspoon baking powder

Heat oil in a large skillet over medium heat. Add bell pepper and green onion; cook until barely tender. Remove from heat and stir in parsley, lemon juice, salt, sugar, oregano, cumin, pepper and corn; set aside to cool.

In a large bowl, beat cream and egg yolks. Stir in flour and baking powder. Stir in corn mixture. In a medium bowl, beat egg whites until stiff, then fold into corn mixture. Drop batter by ¼-cupsful onto a hot, greased griddle or skillet and cook until lightly browned on each side.

Folkestone Inn

The Folkestone Inn is located in a grove of giant Norway spruce trees, beside a mountain brook in the Deep Creek area of Great Smoky Mountains National Park, on the quieter, softer side of the Smokies. The inn is two miles north of Bryson City, a sleepy little mountain community of 1,400 people that offers peace and quiet amidst a wealth of natural scenery and outdoor activities.

Originally a 1920s mountain farmhouse, all guest rooms have claw-foot tubs and some feature a Celeste fireplace and/or a balcony or deck.

INNKEEPERS:	Peggy Myles & Kay Creighton
ADDRESS:	101 Folkestone Road
	Bryson City, North Carolina 28713
TELEPHONE:	(828) 488-2730; (888) 812-3385
E-MAIL:	innkeeper@folkestone.com
WEBSITE:	www.folkestone.com
ROOMS:	10 Rooms; Private baths
CHILDREN:	Children age 10 and older welcome
ANIMALS:	Dogs and horses welcome; Resident cats
HANDICAPPED:	Not handicapped accessible
DIETARY NEEDS:	Will accommodate guests' special dietary needs

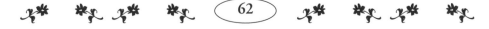

Corn Fritters

Makes 48 Small Fritters

"Soft and creamy on the inside and crisp on the outside, these fritters are best when served warm, right out of the fryer." ~ Innkeeper, Folkestone Inn

Vegetable oil (for frying)
2   **large eggs**
¼   **cup milk**
¼   **cup canned corn liquid or water**
1   **tablespoon butter, melted**
1   **(16-ounce) can corn, drained (liquid reserved)**
2   **cups all-purpose flour**
2   **teaspoons baking powder**
¾   **teaspoon salt**
¼   **teaspoon black pepper**
2   **tablespoons white sugar**
Powdered sugar, for serving
Maple syrup, for serving

Heat 2 inches of oil in an electric skillet or deep-fryer to 350°F. In a large bowl, beat eggs until light. Add milk, corn liquid or water and butter; mix well. Add corn and mix thoroughly. Add flour, baking powder, salt, pepper and white sugar; mix just until dry ingredients are moistened.

Drop batter by rounded teaspoonsful into oil and cook for 2-3 minutes per side, until nicely browned. Drain fritters on paper towels and sprinkle with powdered sugar. Serve with maple syrup.

Old North Durham Inn

Come enjoy the hospitality of the Old North Durham Inn, a restored, early 1900s Colonial Revival home, honored with the Durham Historic Preservation Society's "Architectural Conservation Citation." The inn is located across the street from the house used in the movie "Bull Durham" and a mile from Duke University, the Durham Bulls Ballpark and the historic Carolina Theatre. In 1992, Innkeeper Jim Vickery won the name-the-mascot contest for the Durham Bulls and won free tickets for life to the team's home games which are available and complimentary to inn guests.

INNKEEPERS:	Debbie & Jim Vickery
ADDRESS:	922 North Mangum Street
	Durham, North Carolina 27701
TELEPHONE:	(919) 683-1885
E-MAIL:	dvick1885@aol.com
WEBSITE:	www.bbonline.com/nc/oldnorth
ROOMS:	3 Rooms; 1 Suite; Private baths
CHILDREN:	Welcome
ANIMALS:	Not allowed; Resident dog
HANDICAPPED:	Not handicapped accessible
DIETARY NEEDS:	Will accommodate guests' special dietary needs

Mom's Squash Fritters

Makes About 12 Fritters

"This is a great recipe for using all that squash that seems to pile up during the summer." ~ Innkeeper, Old North Durham Inn

1	egg
⅓	cup milk
1	tablespoon vegetable oil
1	cup all-purpose flour
½	teaspoon salt
1	tablespoon sugar
1	teaspoon baking powder
2	medium yellow squash

Vegetable shortening, for frying

Heat enough shortening to fill an electric skillet ¼-inch-deep to 375°F. In a small bowl, combine egg, milk and oil. In a large bowl, combine flour, salt, sugar and baking powder. Just before cooking, grate squash and stir into flour mixture. Stir in egg mixture. Drop batter by heaping tablespoonsful into shortening. Cook fritters until puffy and light brown on each side.

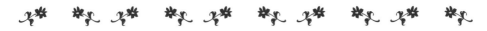

Lois Jane's Riverview Inn

Lois Jane's Riverview Inn is owned and operated by fourth generation, direct descendants of the builder. Constructed in 1891, the home was faithfully restored in 1995 and furnished with traditional period furniture and accessories, many of which are family heirlooms.

Enjoy the breeze on the riverside porches while watching the ships go by. Stroll along the River Walk to antique shops, restaurants, the North Carolina Maritime Museum and other interesting sites in this quaint little town that was settled more than 200 years ago.

INNKEEPERS: Carolyn Davis
ADDRESS: 106 West Bay Street
                 Southport, North Carolina 28461
TELEPHONE: (910) 457-6701
E-MAIL: frontdesk@loisjanes.com
WEBSITE: www.loisjanes.com
ROOMS: 4 Rooms; 1 Suite; Private & shared baths
CHILDREN: Children age 12 and older welcome
ANIMALS: Not allowed
HANDICAPPED: Not handicapped accessible
DIETARY NEEDS: Will accommodate guests' special dietary needs

Nana's Belgian Waffles

Makes 4 Servings

"These waffles are a winner. The recipe has been handed down from generation to generation." ~ Innkeeper, Lois Jane's Riverview Inn

4	large eggs, separated
3	tablespoons butter, melted and cooled
½	teaspoon vanilla extract
1	cup all-purpose flour
½	teaspoon salt

Whipped cream, for serving
1   cup sliced strawberries, for serving

In a medium bowl, beat egg yolks. Mix in butter and vanilla. In a small bowl, combine flour and salt; add to egg yolk mixture and mix well. In a separate bowl, beat egg whites until stiff peaks form; fold into egg yolk mixture. Bake in a preheated Belgian waffle iron until golden brown. Serve with whipped cream and strawberries.

Bed & Breakfast at Laurel Ridge

The peacefulness of the country and 26 acres of gardens, woodland and pastures await you at Laurel Ridge. A long, wooded drive brings you to the inn which is surrounded by a large and beautiful stand of native mountain laurel. The moment you arrive and take a deep breath of clean country air, you'll relax. The hectic workaday world will seem far away.

Stroll through the perennial garden, the sight of many weddings, or take a walk on a trail through the forest that leads to the Rocky River. Deer graze in the early morning or evening in the pasture.

INNKEEPERS:	David Simmons
ADDRESS:	3188 Silver City Snow Camp Road
	Silver City, North Carolina 27344
TELEPHONE:	(919) 742-6049; (800) 742-6049
E-MAIL:	davids@pinehurst.net
WEBSITE:	www.laurel-ridge.com
ROOMS:	2 Rooms; 1 Suite; 1 Cottage; Private baths
CHILDREN:	Children age 10 and older welcome
ANIMALS:	Not allowed; Resident cats
HANDICAPPED:	Handicapped accessible
DIETARY NEEDS:	Will accommodate guests' special dietary needs

Blueberry Basil Cornmeal Waffles

Makes 10 to 12 Waffles

3	tablespoons minced fresh basil
1½	cups cornmeal
½	cup all-purpose flour
¼	cup sugar
½	teaspoon salt
1	teaspoon baking powder
1	teaspoon baking soda
2	eggs, separated
2	cups buttermilk
1	teaspoon vanilla extract
1	stick butter, melted
1	cup blueberries

In a large bowl, combine basil, cornmeal, flour, sugar, salt, baking powder and baking soda. In a medium bowl, mix egg yolks, buttermilk, vanilla and butter until combined. Add buttermilk mixture to cornmeal mixture; mix well. In a separate bowl, beat egg whites until stiff, then fold into batter. Fold in blueberries. Bake waffles until golden brown. Serve with toppings of choice.

French Toast, Bread Puddings, Blintzes & Crêpes

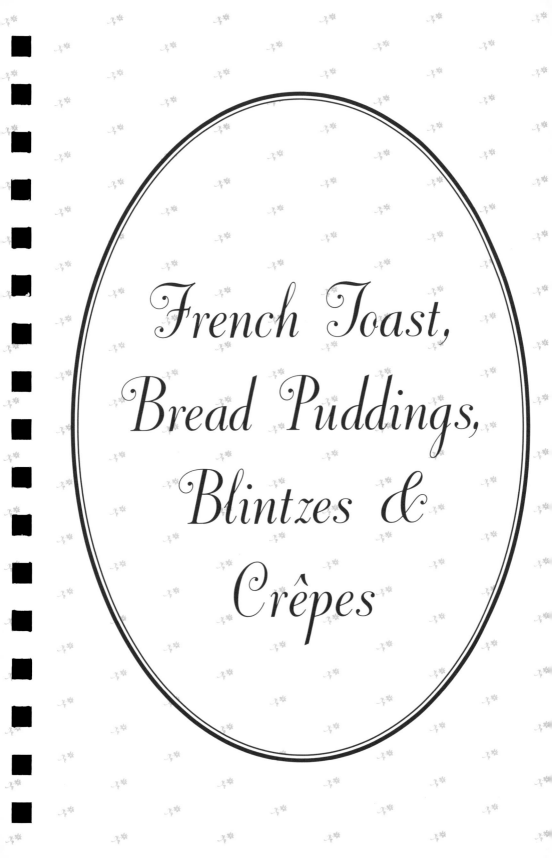

French Toast, Bread Puddings, Blintzes & Crêpes

1902 Turnpike House

The 1902 Turnpike House offers individually decorated, comfortable rooms featuring private baths, down comforters and more. The Sugar Mountain Room is named after a nearby ski and golf resort. It is a cozy, cheerful room with custom-upholstered chairs and ottoman and a spa tub. There is a private entrance off the deck near the hot tub and a sitting area with a bunk bed with a full-size futon bed beneath and twin bed above.

"The beauty of your lovely home was exceeded only by your hospitality. We've never slept so well!" ~ Guests, 1902 Turnpike House

INNKEEPERS:	Paul & Cindy Goedhart
ADDRESS:	317 Old Turnpike Road
	Banner Elk, North Carolina 28604
TELEPHONE:	(828) 898-5611; (888) 802-4487
E-MAIL:	info@1902turnpikehouse.com
WEBSITE:	www.1902turnpikehouse.com
ROOMS:	7 Rooms; Private baths
CHILDREN:	Children age 10 and older welcome
ANIMALS:	Not allowed; Resident dog
HANDICAPPED:	Not handicapped accessible
DIETARY NEEDS:	Will accommodate guests' special dietary needs

Bananas Foster French Toast

Makes 8 Servings

"A delicious combination of a favorite breakfast and a popular dessert. It freezes and reheats well too!" ~ Innkeeper, 1902 Turnpike House Bed & Breakfast

1	stick butter
1	cup packed brown sugar
1	teaspoon cinnamon
¼	teaspoon nutmeg
½	cup banana liqueur
5	bananas, halved lengthwise
¾	cup dark rum
6	eggs
1½	cups milk
½	teaspoon vanilla extract
½	teaspoon banana extract
8	(1- to 1½-inch-thick) slices Hawaiian sweet bread

Maple syrup, for serving

Grease an 8x12-inch baking dish. Melt butter in a large skillet over medium heat. Add brown sugar, cinnamon and nutmeg; cook, stirring, until sugar dissolves. Add banana liqueur and bananas; cook for 4 minutes, turning bananas once. Add rum and carefully light it with a long match. Gently shake pan back and forth until flame goes out (if you need to put out the flame, simply cover the pan with a lid). Put bananas cut-side-down in baking dish. Pour enough pan sauce over bananas to not quite cover them (reserve remaining pan sauce for serving).

In a large bowl, beat eggs, milk and vanilla and banana extracts. Soak bread in egg mixture, then put bread on top of bananas. Pour remaining egg mixture over bread, cover and refrigerate for 2 hours or overnight. When ready to bake, bring French toast to near room temperature. Preheat oven to 375°F and bake French toast for 30-35 minutes. Let stand for 5 minutes, then invert onto a cutting board. Slice and serve with whipped cream and a mixture of reserved pan sauce and maple syrup.

Cedar Crest Victorian Inn

The Cedar Crest Victorian Inn is housed in one of the largest and most opulent residences surviving from Asheville's 1890s boom period. Built in 1891 for Confederate officer William E. Breese, this incredible mansion was once a focal point for the city's wealthy and affluent.

The impressive Queen Anne architecture is surpassed only by the breathtaking interior woodwork and antique furnishings. Guests are truly given the opportunity to step back in time, while enjoying all the luxuries and conveniences of the present.

INNKEEPERS:	Bruce & Rita Wightman
ADDRESS:	674 Biltmore Avenue
	Asheville, North Carolina 28803
TELEPHONE:	(828) 252-1389; (800) 252-0310
E-MAIL:	stay@cedarcrestvictorianinn.com
WEBSITE:	www.cedarcrestvictorianinn.com
ROOMS:	8 Rooms; 4 Suites; 1 Cottage; Private baths
CHILDREN:	Children age 10 and older welcome
ANIMALS:	Not allowed
HANDICAPPED:	Not handicapped accessible
DIETARY NEEDS:	Will accommodate guests' special dietary needs

Autumn Apple French Toast

Makes 12 Servings

1	stick butter
1	cup packed brown sugar
2	tablespoons corn syrup
4	cups chopped (1-inch pieces) peeled Granny Smith apple
1½	loaves cinnamon-raisin bread, cubed
1	(8-ounce) package cream cheese, frozen and shaved*
12	large eggs
1	cup half & half
1	teaspoon vanilla extract

Grease a 9x13-inch glass baking dish. Heat butter, brown sugar and corn syrup in a saucepan over medium-low heat until entire surface is bubbly. Pour butter mixture into a baking dish. Top with apples. Spread bread over apples. Scatter cream cheese over bread. Whisk together eggs, half & half and vanilla; pour over ingredients in baking dish. Cover and refrigerate for at least 1 hour or overnight.

Preheat oven to 350°F. Cover baking dish with foil and bake for 20 minutes. Remove foil and bake for 30-40 minutes more.

*Note: Freezing the cream cheese makes it easier to shave or thinly slice it – a vegetable peeler works well for this.

Chateau on the Mountain

Bed & Breakfast
Chateau
ON THE MOUNTAIN

Perched high atop Hooper's Creek Valley, the Chateau on the Mountain combines old world charm and elegance with modern conveniences and amenities. The inn's mission is to pamper guests with every luxury and service so that their experience will always exceed their expectations and their reaction will be an ongoing "wow!"

Amenities include walking sticks, luxurious robes, Victorian soaps, fluffy towels and a refrigerator with complimentary beverages. Full concierge service helps make this a most enjoyable bed & breakfast experience.

INNKEEPERS:	Jeanne & Lee Yudin
ADDRESS:	1048 Sandy Flat Mountain Road
	Fletcher, North Carolina 28732
TELEPHONE:	(828) 651-9810; (888) 591-6281
E-MAIL:	innkeepers@chateauonthemountain.com
WEBSITE:	www.chateauonthemountain.com
ROOMS:	3 Rooms; 3 Suites; Private baths
CHILDREN:	Welcome
ANIMALS:	Not allowed
HANDICAPPED:	Handicapped accessible
DIETARY NEEDS:	Will accommodate guests' special dietary needs

French Toast à la Sacre Coeur

Makes 3 to 6 Servings

"My husband would often make me French toast on the weekend (before we owned our inn). One day he just experimented and this was the result. It is his version of a Monte Cristo and our guests love it!" ~ Innkeeper, Chateau on the Mountain

6　　large eggs
¾　　cup half & half or milk
Pinch of black pepper
Pinch of cinnamon plus extra, for garnish
6　　thick slices bread
1　　tablespoon butter plus more as needed
6　　medium-thick slices ham
6　　slices mozzarella or Monterey Jack cheese
Powdered sugar, for garnish
Fresh or frozen (thawed) berries, for garnish
Fruit flavored syrup, warmed, for serving

Beat eggs, half & half, pepper and cinnamon until fluffy. Dip bread in egg mixture, turning to soak each side. Melt 1 tablespoon of butter in a skillet over medium heat. Add bread and cook until browned on one side. Turn and cook until second side is halfway cooked. Top with a slice of ham and a slice of cheese and cook until French toast is browned and cheese is slightly melted. Repeat with remaining ingredients. Decorate a serving platter with a sprinkling of powdered sugar and cinnamon along the sides and over the French toast. Garnish with berries and serve with warm fruit syrup.

Note: This would make a great savory dish using Gruyère or Swiss cheese and omitting the sweet ingredients.

The Boxley

T he Boxley is a historic Greek and Federal-style home, the result of three stages of construction. The first one-story structure pre-dates Madison (circa 1785) and contends as the town's oldest structure. The earlier portion of the two-story house was erected in 1825. In the early 1830s, a two-story Greek Revival "L" with another two-story pediment porch supported by monumental Ionic columns was added to the west end of the earlier two-story block. In 1930, the third stage of construction added a sunporch, bathroom and an additional hall and staircase to connect to the main house.

INNKEEPERS:	JoAnn & Monte McIntosh
ADDRESS:	117 East Hunter Street
	Madison, North Carolina 27025
TELEPHONE:	(336) 427-0453; (800) 429-3516
E-MAIL:	info@greensboro-inn.com
WEBSITE:	www.boxleybedandbreakfast.com
ROOMS:	3 Rooms; 1 Cottage; Private baths
CHILDREN:	Welcome
ANIMALS:	Not allowed; Resident dog
HANDICAPPED:	Not handicapped accessible
DIETARY NEEDS:	Will accommodate guests' special dietary needs

Strawberry French Toast

Makes 2 Servings

2   large eggs
¼   cup milk
6   slices bread, crusts removed
1   (8-ounce) container strawberry cream cheese, softened
Sliced strawberries
2   tablespoons butter
Powdered sugar, for garnish
Maple syrup, for serving

Beat eggs and milk in a shallow dish. Spread 1 side of each slice of bread with cream cheese. Put strawberries on each of 3 slices of bread. Sandwich with remaining 3 slices of bread. Dip each sandwich in egg mixture, turning to coat each side. Melt butter in a large skillet over medium heat. Add sandwiches and cook until golden brown on each side. Serve 1½ sandwiches per person. Dust with powdered sugar and serve with maple syrup.

The Trott House Inn

Located in Newton, the county seat of Catawba County, the Trott House Inn gives guests a chance to enjoy such local attractions as the Blue Ridge Parkway and the Hickory Furniture Mart and Hickory Antiques Mall with over 100 retailers and beautiful antiques and collectible Barbies. In winter, there is skiing only one hour away in the bordering mountains.

After a busy day, return to the inn and pamper yourself with an afternoon snack, where you can meet fellow guests, chat with your host or just relax in the pleasant luxury of the two sitting rooms.

INNKEEPERS:	Anne Stedman
ADDRESS:	802 North Main Avenue
	Newton, North Carolina 28658
TELEPHONE:	(828) 465-0404; (877) 435-7994
E-MAIL:	rents40@aol.com
WEBSITE:	www.trotthouse.com
ROOMS:	4 Rooms; 1 Suite; Private baths
CHILDREN:	Children age 12 and older welcome
ANIMALS:	Not allowed; Resident dog
HANDICAPPED:	Not handicapped accessible
DIETARY NEEDS:	Will accommodate guests' special dietary needs

Macadamia Nut French Toast

Makes 4 to 6 Servings

Plan ahead, this French toast needs to be started the night before.

1	(16-ounce) loaf Italian bread, cut into 1-inch-thick slices
4	large eggs, lightly beaten
¼	cup sugar
¼	teaspoon nutmeg plus extra, for garnish
⅔	cup orange juice
⅓	cup milk
½	teaspoon vanilla extract
1	stick plus 3 tablespoons butter or margarine, melted
½	cup chopped macadamia nuts

Powdered sugar, for garnish

Maple syrup, for serving

Fit bread in a single layer in a lightly greased 9x13-inch baking pan. Mix eggs, sugar, nutmeg, orange juice, milk and vanilla; pour over bread. Cover and refrigerate overnight, turning bread once.

The next day, preheat oven to 400°F. Pour butter in a 15x10-inch jellyroll pan. Place bread in a single layer on top of butter. Bake for 10 minutes. Sprinkle with nuts and bake for 10 minutes more. Sprinkle with powdered sugar and nutmeg, if desired. Serve immediately with maple syrup.

Colonial Pines Inn

At the Colonial Pines Inn, you will find a variety of accommodations and settings perfect for a memorable mountain vacation. Meticulous attention to detail is evident at every turn. You see it in the warmth of the knotty pine, in the eclectic blend of books and accessories, in the comfortable antique furnishings and rugs and in the sitting rooms with views of the surrounding mountains and the lush gardens.

Whether you want a quiet mountain getaway or a romantic escape, you will find exactly what you are looking for at the Colonial Pines Inn.

INNKEEPERS:	Chris & Donna Alley
ADDRESS:	541 Hickory Street
	Highlands, North Carolina 28741
TELEPHONE:	(828) 526-2060
E-MAIL:	sleeptight@colonialpinesinn.com
WEBSITE:	www.colonialpinesinn.com
ROOMS:	3 Rooms; 3 Suites; 2 Cottages; Private baths
CHILDREN:	Call ahead
ANIMALS:	Not allowed
HANDICAPPED:	Not handicapped accessible
DIETARY NEEDS:	Will accommodate guests' special dietary needs

Baked Blueberry French Toast

Makes 6 Servings

"We serve this dish every Sunday morning with fresh seasonal fruit and spicy sausage patties. Plan ahead, this French toast needs to be started the night before." ~ Innkeeper, Colonial Pines Inn

10	slices white, wheat or other favorite bread
½	(8-ounce) package cream cheese
¾	cup fresh blueberries
12	eggs, beaten well
¼	cup maple syrup plus extra, for serving
2½	cups whole milk

Spray a 9x13-inch baking dish with non-stick cooking spray. Tear bread into pieces. Scatter ½ of bread in baking dish. Pinch off ½-inch pieces of cream cheese and scatter over bread. Scatter blueberries over cream cheese. Top with remaining bread. Mix eggs, ¼ cup of maple syrup and milk; pour over ingredients in baking dish. Cover and refrigerate overnight.

The next day, preheat oven to 325°F. Bake French toast for 1 hour, then broil lightly to brown top. Serve with maple syrup.

Colby House

Breakfasts at the Colby House are prepared with ingredients such as real butter and fresh herbs, fruits and vegetables. A morning menu may include poached pears with berry compote, cinnamon sour cream coffee cake and an Irish frittata with sausage. Fresh baked cookies are available all the time. Mouth-watering varieties include almond sandies, orange almond biscotti, cranberry chocolate chip and double chocolate walnut brownies.

"We now have first-hand knowledge of the word 'gracious.' We loved the cottage, the gardens, the lovely breakfasts and precious treatment." ~ Guest

INNKEEPERS:	Peter & Bonnie Marsh
ADDRESS:	230 Pearson Drive
	Asheville, North Carolina 28801
TELEPHONE:	(828) 253-5644; (800) 982-2118
E-MAIL:	colbyhouse@cs.com
WEBSITE:	www.colbyhouse.com
ROOMS:	4 Rooms; 1 Cottage; Private baths
CHILDREN:	Call ahead
ANIMALS:	Not allowed
HANDICAPPED:	Not handicapped accessible
DIETARY NEEDS:	Will accommodate guests' special dietary needs

Apple Cobbler French Toast

Makes 8 Servings

Plan ahead, this French toast needs to be started the night before.

1	loaf French bread, cut into 1-inch cubes
4	eggs
1	cup milk
¼	teaspoon baking powder
1	teaspoon vanilla extract
3	large Granny Smith apples, peeled, cored and sliced
½	cup packed brown sugar
1	teaspoon cinnamon
2	tablespoons butter, melted

Maple syrup, for serving

Put bread in a 9x13-inch baking dish. Whisk together eggs, milk, baking powder and vanilla; pour over bread and toss gently to coat bread. Cover and refrigerate overnight.

The next day, preheat oven to 450°F. Put apples in a greased 9x13-inch baking dish. Combine brown sugar and cinnamon; sprinkle over apples. Arrange bread on top of apples. Brush with butter. Bake for 25 minutes. Serve with warm maple syrup.

The Yellow House

The Yellow House
Waynesville

The Yellow House on Plott Creek Road is located just outside of Waynesville, in the country, at an elevation of 3,000 feet. The inn is 25 miles from Asheville, 10 minutes from the Blue Ridge Parkway and 20 minutes from the Great Smoky Mountain National Park. Nearby are Cataloochee Ski Area, Maggie Valley and the Pisgah National Forest.

At the inn, you will enjoy the restful, relaxing and romantic mood of the Yellow House, as well as the mountain atmosphere of the Blue Ridge and Great Smoky Mountains of North Carolina.

INNKEEPERS:	Donna & Stephen Shea
ADDRESS:	89 Oakview Drive
	Waynesville, North Carolina 28786
TELEPHONE:	(828) 452-0991; (800) 563-1236
E-MAIL:	info@theyellowhouse.com
WEBSITE:	www.theyellowhouse.com
ROOMS:	10 Rooms; Private baths
CHILDREN:	Children age 12 and older welcome
ANIMALS:	Not allowed
HANDICAPPED:	Not handicapped accessible
DIETARY NEEDS:	Will accommodate guests' special dietary needs

Outrageous French Toast

Makes 8 Servings

Plan ahead, this French toast needs to be started the night before.

1	cup packed light brown sugar
1	tablespoon light Karo syrup
5	tablespoons butter
1	teaspoon cinnamon
16	slices whole-wheat bread, crusts removed
5	eggs
1½	cups milk
1	teaspoon vanilla extract

Sour cream, for serving
Fresh or frozen strawberries, for serving

Grease a 9x13-inch baking pan. Combine brown sugar, Karo syrup, butter and cinnamon in a small saucepan over low heat; cook, stirring, until sugar is melted and combined. Pour brown sugar mixture into baking pan and spread evenly. Top with 8 slices of bread, squeezing or cutting to fit if needed. Top with remaining bread, squeezing or cutting to fit if needed. Beat eggs, milk and vanilla; pour over bread, cover and refrigerate overnight.

The next morning, preheat oven to 350°F. Bake French toast for 45 minutes. Cut into 8 pieces, then invert each serving onto a plate, sugar-side-up. Serve topped with a dollop of sour cream and strawberries.

Katherine's

While innkeeper Ineke Strongman was raised in the Netherlands, it may be her lifetime of traveling the world that has contributed most in creating the high style and rich detail found at Katherine's Bed & Breakfast. The inn reflects the many places she has visited in her years of exploring the globe, while her skill in decorating and her talent for historic restoration have combined to create this elegant and comfortable inn.

Each bedroom is a picture-perfect gem with private bath, down comforter, plush robes, fireplace and a special teddy bear to welcome you.

INNKEEPERS:	Ineke Strongman & Michael Pewther
ADDRESS:	43 Watauga Street
	Asheville, North Carolina 28801
TELEPHONE:	(828) 236-9494; (888) 325-3190
E-MAIL:	info@katherinesbandb.com
WEBSITE:	www.katherinesbandb.com
ROOMS:	5 Rooms; 1 Suite; Private baths
CHILDREN:	Children age 12 and older welcome
ANIMALS:	Not allowed; Resident cat
HANDICAPPED:	Not handicapped accessible
DIETARY NEEDS:	Will accommodate guests' special dietary needs

Cinnamon Toasty Delight

Makes 4 Servings

"This is a tasty and different approach to French toast. I serve one and one-half slices per person, cut on the diagonal, which is plenty as I use thicker bread." ~ Innkeeper, Katherine's Bed & Breakfast

2	cups pancake mix
1½	cups water
1	teaspoon vanilla extract
¼	teaspoon cinnamon
2	tablespoons butter, divided
2	tablespoons vegetable oil, divided
8	thick slices cinnamon-raisin bread
2	bananas, sliced
¼	cup chopped pecans

Powdered sugar, for garnish
Fresh sliced strawberries, for garnish
Maple syrup, for serving

In a large bowl, whisk together pancake mix, water, vanilla and cinnamon. Melt ½ tablespoon of butter with ½ tablespoon of oil in a large skillet over medium heat. Dip bread in pancake mix mixture, turning to coat each side. Cook bread for 2 minutes per side, until golden. Repeat with remaining bread, adding more butter and oil as needed. Top each serving with bananas and pecans and sprinkle with powdered sugar. Garnish with strawberries and serve with maple syrup.

Biltmore Village Inn

The closest of Asheville's bed & breakfast inns to the Biltmore Estate, the Biltmore Village Inn is located on top of Reed Hill, above Biltmore Village. The entrance to the Biltmore Estate can be seen from the inn's tower sitting area.

From there and the porch, you can see why Samuel Reed, George Vanderbilt's lawyer, situated his house here after he sold Asheville's first multi-millionaire the property for Biltmore Village. It commanded a 360-degree view of the mountains and overlooked the village and the Swannanoa River valley below.

INNKEEPERS:	**Ripley Hotch & Owen Sullivan**
ADDRESS:	119 Dodge Street
	Asheville, North Carolina 28803
TELEPHONE:	(828) 274-8707; (866) 274-8779
E-MAIL:	info@biltmorevillageinn.com
WEBSITE:	www.biltmorevillageinn.com
ROOMS:	4 Rooms; 2 Suites; 1 Cottage; Private baths
CHILDREN:	Children age 12 and older welcome
ANIMALS:	Dogs under 45 pounds welcome; Resident dog
HANDICAPPED:	Not handicapped accessible
DIETARY NEEDS:	Will accommodate guests' special dietary needs

Raspberry Orange Croissants

Makes 6 Servings

Plan ahead, this dish needs to be started the night before.

6	medium croissants, halved lengthwise
1	(8-ounce) package cream cheese, softened
1	cup fresh or frozen raspberries
8	eggs
½	cup sugar
1	cup half & half
1	teaspoon nutmeg
1	teaspoon almond extract
½	cup orange marmalade
¼	cup orange juice

Grease or lightly oil a 7x11-inch or 9x13-inch baking dish. Spread croissant halves with cream cheese. Arrange some raspberries on top of each croissant bottom, then sandwich with croissant tops. Put croissants in baking dish.

In a medium bowl, beat eggs. Add sugar, half & half, nutmeg and almond extract; mix well and pour over croissants. In a small bowl, mix marmalade and orange juice; spoon over croissants. Cover and refrigerate overnight.

The next morning, preheat oven to 350°F. Bake croissants for about 40 minutes, until custard is puffy and slightly browned. Cut apart to serve.

Flint Street Inns

The Flint Street Inns reflect the grace and serenity that are a special part of Southern hospitality. The comfort of the rooms is enhanced by the pleasant parlors and living rooms. The guest bedrooms are old fashioned and charming, furnished with antiques and collectibles, and each with its own personality. There is a wonderful use of color in the wallpaper, quilts and comforters.

Rooms have special touches, such as fresh flowers and an array of reading material from novels to magazines.

INNKEEPERS:	Rick, Lynne & Marion Vogel
ADDRESS:	116 Flint Street
	Asheville, North Carolina 28801
TELEPHONE:	(828) 253-6723; (800) 234-8172
E-MAIL:	flintstreetinns@cs.com
WEBSITE:	www.flintstreetinns.com
ROOMS:	8 Rooms; Private baths
CHILDREN:	Children age 14 and older welcome
ANIMALS:	Not allowed
HANDICAPPED:	Not handicapped accessible
DIETARY NEEDS:	Will accommodate guests' special dietary needs

Breakfast Bread Pudding with Berry Sauce

Makes 16 Servings

This recipe can be halved and baked in a 9x9-inch pan.

2   quarts half & half
½   cup sugar, divided
1   teaspoon vanilla extract
Grated zest of 2 oranges
14   egg yolks
1   whole egg
1½   (1-pound) loaves day-old bread, broken into walnut-size pieces

Berry sauce:
1½   cups sugar
3   tablespoons cornstarch
1½   cups water
1   (16-ounce) package favorite frozen berries, thawed and drained well
1½   tablespoons butter

Preheat oven to 350°F. Heat half & half, ¼ cup of sugar, vanilla and orange zest in a saucepan over medium heat (do not boil); remove from heat; let stand for 10 minutes. In a stainless steel bowl, whip egg yolks, egg and remaining ¼ cup sugar. Over low heat, mix egg yolk mixture into half & half mixture. Put bread in an ungreased 9x13-inch baking pan. Pour egg mixture over bread; let stand for 10 minutes. Put baking dish in a larger pan with 1 inch of warm water. Bake for 40-45 minutes, until custard is set and lightly browned. Remove from water bath and cool on a wire rack. Cut into 8 pieces, then cut each piece diagonally in half. Top with berry sauce.

For the berry sauce: Combine sugar and cornstarch in saucepan over medium heat. Whisk in water and bring to a boil. Lower heat and simmer for 5 minutes. Add berries and butter; simmer for 10 minutes. (This sauce keeps well covered and refrigerated or frozen.)

Chateau on the Mountain

Bed & Breakfast

S ome call it the master suite, the honeymoon suite or the presidential suite. At Chateau on the Mountain, it is called the Biltmore Suite and it is deserving of the name. Fit for a king and sure to make his companion feel like a queen, guests report that the more than 950-square-feet of luxury make it hard to leave. A king-size bed with a 17-inch-thick mattress, down comforter and the finest linens make sweet dreams a certainty.

There's a large porch to catch the morning rays and a balcony to enjoy the sunset. Also included are a steam shower and a very romantic Jacuzzi tub.

INNKEEPERS:	Jeanne & Lee Yudin
ADDRESS:	1048 Sandy Flat Mountain Road
	Fletcher, North Carolina 28732
TELEPHONE:	(828) 651-9810; (888) 591-6281
E-MAIL:	innkeepers@chateauonthemountain.com
WEBSITE:	www.chateauonthemountain.com
ROOMS:	3 Rooms; 3 Suites; Private baths
CHILDREN:	Welcome
ANIMALS:	Not allowed
HANDICAPPED:	Handicapped accessible
DIETARY NEEDS:	Will accommodate guests' special dietary needs

Breakfast in Bed
Biltmore Blintzes

Makes 3 to 4 Servings

1½   cups all-purpose flour
⅛   teaspoon salt
2   eggs, beaten
1   cup water plus more, as needed
6   ounces ricotta cheese
⅓   cup cooked berries (drained) or jelly

Flambé berry sauce:
2   cups frozen berries, thawed
1   cup packed brown sugar
½   cup Kirsch or other fruit liqueur plus extra, for flaming

Preheat oven to 350°F. In a medium bowl, mix flour and salt. In a small bowl, mix eggs and 1 cup of water. Add egg mixture to flour mixture, a little at a time, mixing well after each addition until smooth. Slowly add enough additional water to form a thin batter.

Add batter by ¼-cupful to a non-stick or oiled 9-inch skillet over medium heat (amount will depend on pan size and desired thickness of blintzes). Turn skillet in a circle as blintz cooks. Stack cooked blintzes between layers of waxed paper. (Adjust heat and batter as necessary – the batter will thicken and more water will be needed. It's okay if the first blintz does not turn out well, usually the heat and skillet need to stabilize and the first blintz is not used.) Spread each blintz with ricotta cheese and berries or jelly. Roll up blintzes and serve with berry sauce or powdered sugar and whipped cream.

For the berry sauce: Combine berries and brown sugar in a saucepan over medium heat; cook until most of liquid is gone. Add more sugar, if desired. Add ½ cup of Kirsch and cook until heated through. Pour enough Kirsch into a large metal cooking spoon to fill. Flame liqueur with a match and carefully add lighted liqueur to berries. Pour sauce over blintzes.

Albemarle Inn

The Albemarle Inn, a magnificently restored 1907 Greek Revival mansion, is located in park-like grounds in Asheville's famed Grove Park district. Luxuriously appointed rooms pamper guests with period furnishings, fine linens, down quilts and baths with claw-foot tubs.

The formal parlor includes a blazing fireplace and fine antiques, surrounded by original oak wainscoting and a sweeping staircase leading to guest rooms. Gourmet breakfasts graced with crisp linen and gleaming silver are served in the candlelit dining room or the sunporch overlooking an English garden.

INNKEEPERS:	Cathy & Larry Sklar
ADDRESS:	86 Edgemont Road
	Asheville, North Carolina 28801
TELEPHONE:	(828) 255-0027; (800) 621-7435
E-MAIL:	info@albemarleinn.com
WEBSITE:	www.albemarleinn.com
ROOMS:	9 Rooms; 2 Suites; Private baths
CHILDREN:	Children age 12 and older welcome
ANIMALS:	Not allowed; Resident dogs
HANDICAPPED:	Not handicapped accessible
DIETARY NEEDS:	Will accommodate guests' special dietary needs

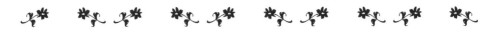

Ruffled Crêpes

Makes 6 Servings

Crêpes:
1¼ cups all-purpose flour
2   tablespoons sugar
Pinch of salt
3   eggs
1½ cups milk
2   tablespoons butter, melted

Filling:
7   eggs
1½ cups milk
½   teaspoon salt
¼   teaspoon black pepper
1   tablespoon all-purpose flour
1   pound bacon, cooked crisp and crumbled
2   cups grated cheddar cheese
Roasted red pepper sauce (see recipe on page 183)

For the crêpes: Blend or mix crêpe ingredients. Let stand for 15 minutes.
Spray a 5-inch, non-stick crêpe or omelet pan with non-stick cooking
spray. Heat pan over medium-high heat. Pour ¼ cup of batter into pan; tilt
quickly to evenly cover bottom of pan. Cook for 30-35 seconds per side.
Stack cooked crêpes between layers of waxed paper. (Crêpes can be made
1 day ahead, stacked, cooled completely, covered and refrigerated.)

For the filling: Preheat oven to 385°F. Spray 12 muffin cups with non-stick
cooking spray. Press 1 crêpe into each muffin cup, lightly ruffling edges (be
careful not to tear crêpes). Combine bacon and cheese; divide among
muffin cups. Combine eggs, milk, salt, pepper and flour; divide among
muffin cups, filling close to top of cups. Bake for 15-20 minutes on lower
rack of oven, until egg mixture is firm and slightly puffed and crêpes are
lightly browned around edges. Carefully loosen crêpe cups from muffin
cups. Put a little roasted red pepper sauce on each plate. Place 2 crêpe cups
of top of sauce. Drizzle with additional sauce and serve.

Turn of the Century Victorian

Whether relaxing or exploring the area's rich history and heritage, the Turn of the Century Victorian Bed & Breakfast provides the perfect home away from home. Guests are welcomed through a magnificent, leaded beveled glass entry featuring copper wheel engraved double doors that lead into an inviting foyer and parlor furnished with period antiques.

Your stay includes a full gourmet breakfast elegantly served in the large formal dining room. Then relax and enjoy your coffee or tea on the lovely wrap-around porch.

INNKEEPERS:	Karen Windate
ADDRESS:	259 South Fulton Street
	Salisbury, North Carolina 28144
TELEPHONE:	(704) 642-1660; (800) 250-5349
E-MAIL:	info@turnofthecenturybb.com
WEBSITE:	www.turnofthecenturybb.com
ROOMS:	3 Rooms; 1 Suite; Private baths
CHILDREN:	Children age 12 and older welcome
ANIMALS:	Not allowed
HANDICAPPED:	Not handicapped accessible
DIETARY NEEDS:	Will accommodate guests' special dietary needs

Crêpes with Mushroom Sauce

Makes 4 Servings

Mushroom sauce:

½	stick butter
3	tablespoons minced onion
8	ounces mushrooms, minced plus sliced mushrooms, for garnish
2	tablespoons all-purpose flour
1	cup half & half
2	tablespoons water
2	tablespoons lemon juice
2	teaspoons chopped parsley
2	teaspoons chopped chives
1	teaspoon cayenne pepper
¼	teaspoon salt

Crêpes and filling:
Crêpes (see recipe on page 97)

2	tablespoons butter
8	large eggs
¼	cup half & half

Salt and pepper, to taste
Chopped fresh tarragon, to taste plus tarragon sprigs, for garnish

For the sauce: Melt butter in a skillet over medium heat. Add onion; cook until soft. Add mushrooms; cook for 10-15 minutes, until moisture is gone. Add flour and mix well. Add half & half, return to heat and bring to a boil. Lower heat and simmer for 2 minutes. Remove from heat. Stir in water, lemon juice, parsley, chives, cayenne and salt; cover and keep warm.

For the crêpes and filling: Prepare crêpes according to recipe directions, using 1 teaspoon of sugar instead of 2 tablespoons. Add ¼ cup of batter to a crêpe pan or a skillet over medium heat; swirl batter to cover pan. Cook until light brown on bottom, turn and cook for a few seconds more. Melt butter in a skillet over medium heat. Beat eggs, half & half, salt, pepper and chopped tarragon; soft scramble eggs. Put 1 crêpe on each plate. Put some eggs in a line down center of each crêpe. Fold sides of crêpe over eggs. Spoon sauce over crêpes. Garnish with sliced mushrooms and tarragon to serve.

Egg Dishes & Breakfast Entrées

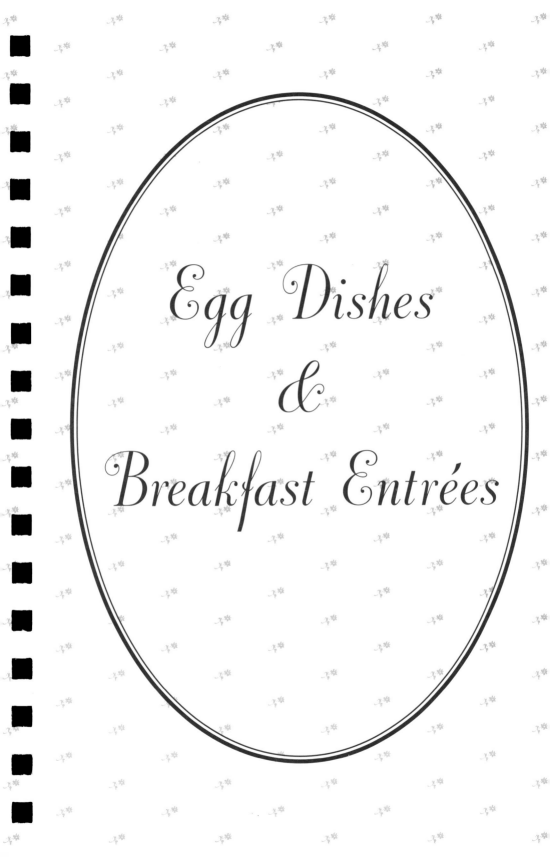

Egg Dishes
&
Breakfast Entrées

1904 Secret Garden

The Secret Garden is a large, turn-of-the-century home once owned by Mayor John Erskine and his poet-wife, Edith Erskine. This circa 1904 residence was "the place" for cotillion dances and large social events hosted by the mayor. Imagine those grand parties while you are enjoying breakfast in the gracious dining room.

Feel the grand elegance of the rooms as you are surrounded with classical and period music. Relax, as even the mayor must have done in times past, as you enjoy the large front porch and the abundance of singing birds.

INNKEEPERS:	Cassandra Clark
ADDRESS:	56 North Main Street
	Weaverville, North Carolina 28787
TELEPHONE:	(828) 658-9317; (800) 797-8211
E-MAIL:	garden56@aol.com
WEBSITE:	www.secretgardennc.com
ROOMS:	3 Rooms; 3 Suites; Private baths
CHILDREN:	Children age 16 and older welcome
ANIMALS:	Not allowed
HANDICAPPED:	Not handicapped accessible
DIETARY NEEDS:	Will accommodate guests' special dietary needs

Black Forest Ham & Egg Cups

Makes 6 Servings

"This has become a signature recipe for the inn. It is always requested by return guests! I serve it with hash browns and fresh tomatoes or asparagus. I serve two egg cups per person." ~ Innkeeper, 1904 Secret Garden Bed & Breakfast

2	tablespoons unsalted butter
½	teaspoon salt
¼	teaspoon black pepper
¾	pound baby bella or portobello mushrooms, chopped
¼	cup finely chopped shallots
2	tablespoons sour cream
1	tablespoon finely chopped fresh tarragon plus extra, for garnish
12	slices Black Forest ham
12	eggs

Preheat oven to 400°F. Melt butter with salt and pepper in a skillet over medium heat. Add mushrooms and shallots; cook for about 10 minutes, until mushrooms are tender and liquid has evaporated. Remove from heat and stir in sour cream and tarragon.

Lightly grease 12 muffin cups. Fit 1 slice of ham in each muffin cup (ham will hang over edges of cups). Divide mushroom mixture among ham cups. Crack 1 egg into each ham cup (be careful not to break yolks).

Bake ham cups until egg whites are cooked but yolks are still runny (not more than 15 minutes). Carefully remove ham cups with a rubber spatula, being sure to keep ham cup intact. Sprinkle with tarragon and serve.

The River Lodge

On a bend in the Tuckasegee River sits the River Lodge, an elegant Smoky Mountain bed & breakfast built with 100-year-old, hand-hewn logs taken from old barns and cabins in the region. The inn is rustic elegance at its best – from the massive stone fireplace to the handmade twig beds and gourmet breakfasts, everything about it is a delight to the senses.

This is mountain lodging that is away from town but close to everything that is great about western North Carolina – the mountains, streams, trails, waterfalls and the never-ending panorama of spectacular scenery.

INNKEEPERS:	Cathy & Anthony Sgambato
ADDRESS:	619 Roy Tritt Road
	Cullowhee, North Carolina 28723
TELEPHONE:	(877) 384-4400
E-MAIL:	cathy@riverlodge-bb.com
WEBSITE:	www.riverlodge-bb.com
ROOMS:	5 Rooms; 1 Suite; Private baths
CHILDREN:	Children age 13 and older welcome
ANIMALS:	Not allowed; Resident dog
HANDICAPPED:	Not handicapped accessible
DIETARY NEEDS:	Will accommodate guests' special dietary needs

Eggs Neptune

Makes 4 Servings

1   teaspoon salt
8   spears fresh asparagus, thick ends trimmed
12   medium shrimp, shelled, cleaned and sliced in half lengthwise
3   tablespoons distilled white vinegar
8   large eggs
4   small croissants, halved lengthwise and toasted lightly
8   thin slices smoked salmon
Fresh dill
4   medium fresh strawberries, sliced and fanned with leaves attached

Hollandaise sauce:
4   egg yolks
1   tablespoon fresh lemon juice
1   stick butter, cut into pieces

Fill a skillet with water. Add salt and bring to a simmer. Add asparagus and cook for about 2 minutes; remove from skillet and set aside. Add shrimp to skillet and cook until barely cooked; remove from pan and set aside. Add vinegar to water in skillet. Break each egg into a saucer and slide into water, taking care not to break yolks. Poach eggs for 3-5 minutes. Put 1 slice of smoked salmon and 1 egg on each croissant half.

Reheat asparagus in simmering water in skillet, then remove. Add shrimp to simmering water and cook just for about 20 seconds, until they begin to curl (do not overcook); remove immediately. Put 1 asparagus spear on one side of each plate. Spoon hollandaise sauce over eggs, letting some sauce drizzle over asparagus. Arrange 6 shrimp halves on top of sauce. Snip dill over eggs with kitchen scissors. Garnish with a fresh strawberry to serve.

For the hollandaise sauce: In a small saucepan over low heat, whisk together egg yolks and lemon juice until combined. Add butter and cook, whisking constantly, until mixture thickens. If sauce is too thick, whisk in a little bit of water. Remove from heat and use immediately.

Folkestone Inn

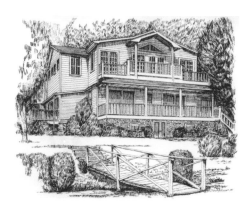

The Folkestone Inn is located in a grove of giant Norway spruce trees, beside a mountain brook in the Deep Creek area of Great Smoky Mountains National Park, on the quieter, softer side of the Smokies. The inn is two miles north of Bryson City, a sleepy little mountain community of 1,400 people that offers peace and quiet amidst a wealth of natural scenery and outdoor activities.

Originally a 1920s mountain farmhouse, all guest rooms have claw-foot tubs and some feature a Celeste fireplace and/or a balcony or deck.

INNKEEPERS:	Peggy Myles & Kay Creighton
ADDRESS:	101 Folkestone Road
	Bryson City, North Carolina 28713
TELEPHONE:	(828) 488-2730; (888) 812-3385
E-MAIL:	innkeeper@folkestone.com
WEBSITE:	www.folkestone.com
ROOMS:	10 Rooms; Private baths
CHILDREN:	Children age 10 and older welcome
ANIMALS:	Dogs and horses welcome; Resident cats
HANDICAPPED:	Not handicapped accessible
DIETARY NEEDS:	Will accommodate guests' special dietary needs

Grits Cakes with Fresh Tomato Sauce & Scrambled Eggs

Makes 8 Servings

Plan ahead, this dish needs to be started the night before.

Grits cakes:
4	cups water
1	cup stone ground grits
1	teaspoon salt
2⅔	tablespoons butter, melted plus extra, for cooking grits cakes
1½	cups grated cheddar cheese

Preheat oven to 350°F. Butter a 9x13-inch glass baking dish. Bring water to a boil. Add grits and salt; simmer for 5-6 minutes. Stir in melted butter and cheese. Pour mixture into baking dish. Bake for 30 minutes, or until top is golden. Cool, cover with foil and refrigerate overnight. The next day, cut grits into 8 squares. Butter a griddle or non-stick skillet over medium heat. Cook grits squares until heated through and crisp on each side.

Fresh tomato sauce & scrambled eggs:
2	tablespoons butter
¼	cup minced onion
1	tablespoon all-purpose flour
1	teaspoon sugar
1	teaspoon salt
Black pepper, to taste	
5-6	tomatoes, peeled, seeded and quartered
16	eggs

Melt butter in a saucepan over medium heat. Add onion and cook until translucent. Stir in flour and cook for 2-3 minutes. Add sugar, salt and pepper. Carefully stir in tomatoes. Lower heat to low, cover and cook until tomatoes are softened, but not mushy. Scramble eggs. Put a grits cake on each plate. Put scrambled eggs to one side of grits cake, leaving about ½-inch between. Pour a ribbon of tomato sauce between and over grits cake and eggs to serve.

1889 WhiteGate Inn & Cottage

The award-winning gardens of the 1889 WhiteGate Inn & Cottage have an extensive collection of unusual plants. These include 18 varieties of Japanese maples and over 300 different varieties of perennials, hostas, roses and herbs. The innkeepers grow dill, thyme, rosemary, oregano and more to flavor the delicious home-cooked breakfasts each morning.

In the greenhouse is a collection of over 1,500 orchids and tropicals. Paths and sitting areas throughout the gardens make it a perfect place to wander or to sit and meditate amidst nature's beauty and abundance.

INNKEEPERS:	Ralph Coffey & Frank Salvo
ADDRESS:	173 East Chestnut Street
	Asheville, North Carolina 28801
TELEPHONE:	(828) 253-2553; (800) 485-3045
E-MAIL:	innkeeper@whitegate.net
WEBSITE:	www.whitegate.net
ROOMS:	2 Rooms; 3 Suites; 1 Cottage; Private baths
CHILDREN:	Children age 15 and older welcome
ANIMALS:	Not allowed
HANDICAPPED:	Not handicapped accessible
DIETARY NEEDS:	Will accommodate guests' special dietary needs

Crab & Artichoke Egg Puff with White Wine Sauce

Makes 4 Servings

Egg puff:
5   eggs, beaten
¼   cup all-purpose flour
½   teaspoon baking powder
1   (8-ounce) carton cottage cheese
2   cups grated Monterey Jack cheese
¼   pound shredded crabmeat (or imitation crabmeat)
6   ounces chopped artichoke hearts (not marinated)
Salt and black pepper, to taste

White wine sauce:
2   tablespoons butter
½   cup white wine
1   tablespoon flour
1   cup half & half
2   tablespoons chopped fresh parsley

For the egg puff: Preheat oven to 350°F. Spray 4 individual ramekins with non-stick cooking spray. Combine all egg puff ingredients and mix well. Divide egg mixture among ramekins. Bake for about 30 minutes, or until golden brown. Drizzle each serving with white wine sauce and serve.

For the white wine sauce: Combine butter and wine in saucepan over medium heat. Bring to a boil. Gradually add flour while whisking briskly. Remove pan from heat and add half & half, whisking until smooth. Fold in parsley. Serve warm.

The Yellow House

the Yellow House
Waynesville

Memories of the rural village of E'staing, France inspired the two-room E'staing Suite. The room's stone fireplace and natural-wood bed, dresser and shutters are reminiscent of a quaint French village. The suite's sitting room, with its wet bar, games, comfortable furnishings and fireplace, is a great place to spend a lazy afternoon.

Both rooms open to a private balcony with a wonderful pine-framed view of the mountains and town. At night, the twinkling town lights create one of the most romantic spots found anywhere – it is a delight for the senses.

INNKEEPERS:	Donna & Stephen Shea
ADDRESS:	89 Oakview Drive
	Waynesville, North Carolina 28786
TELEPHONE:	(828) 452-0991; (800) 563-1236
E-MAIL:	info@theyellowhouse.com
WEBSITE:	www.theyellowhouse.com
ROOMS:	10 Rooms; Private baths
CHILDREN:	Children age 12 and older welcome
ANIMALS:	Not allowed
HANDICAPPED:	Not handicapped accessible
DIETARY NEEDS:	Will accommodate guests' special dietary needs

Chili Cheese Egg Puff

Makes 8 Servings

5   eggs, beaten well
¼   cup all-purpose flour
1   teaspoon salt
1   teaspoon baking powder
1   cup cottage cheese
½   stick butter, melted
1   (4-ounce) can chopped mild green chilies
2   cups grated colby cheese, divided
2   cups grated Monterey Jack cheese, divided

Preheat oven to 350°F. Grease a 7x9-inch glass baking dish. Combine eggs, flour, salt, baking powder, cottage cheese, butter, green chilies, 1 cup of colby cheese and 1 cup of Monterey Jack cheese. Pour mixture into baking dish. Sprinkle with remaining cheeses and bake for 30-45 minutes, until cheese has melted.

The Burke Manor Inn

Located in historic Gibsonville, the Burke Manor Inn Bed & Breakfast is a prestigious, historic inn set on three and one-half acres. The ambiance of the home, combined with exceptional food and service, has created a dining experience that has quickly earned the inn a reputation as a fine dining destination in the area.

"I've stayed in B&B's all over the world and this would be in my very top category. It's really exceptional. All the amenities that focus on service are extraordinary." ~ Maxine Pinson, Editor, *The Innside Scoop*

INNKEEPERS:	Vernon & Lynn Brady
ADDRESS:	303 Burke Street
	Gibsonville, North Carolina 27249
TELEPHONE:	(336) 449-6266; (888) 287-5311
E-MAIL:	info@burkemanor.com
WEBSITE:	www.burkemanor.com
ROOMS:	7 Suites; Private baths
CHILDREN:	Children age 12 and older welcome
ANIMALS:	Not allowed
HANDICAPPED:	Not handicapped accessible
DIETARY NEEDS:	Will accommodate guests' special dietary needs

Baked Chardonnay Cream Eggs

Makes 4 Servings

"Having original and unique breakfasts is one of the tricky parts of running an inn. At the Burke Manor, we try not to "casserole," but to have individual items for each guest. This elegant dish allows for that individual presentation but also has an easy make-ahead preparation. Some guests eat it from the ramekin it's served in, while others open up their croissant and spoon it over." - Innkeeper, The Burke Manor Inn

2	tablespoons butter
1	teaspoon chicken stock paste*
¼	cup Chardonnay wine plus more for additional flavor, if desired
2	tablespoons all-purpose flour
1	cup half & half
1	cup milk
¼	cup grated Parmesan cheese

Salt and black pepper, to taste

8	eggs

Chopped parsley, for garnish

4	croissants, warmed or toasted, for serving

Melt butter in a 2-quart saucepan over medium heat. Stir in chicken stock paste. Stir in wine. Add flour and cook, stirring, until a thick paste is formed. Gradually stir in half & half and milk. Cook, stirring, until thickened. Stir in cheese. Season with salt and pepper. (The recipe can be prepared to this point the night before, covered and refrigerated.)

Preheat oven to 400°F. Spray 4 individual ramekins with non-stick cooking spray. Spoon a small amount of sauce into each ramekin. Crack 2 eggs into each ramekin. Spoon remaining sauce over eggs, leaving yolks partially uncovered to check for doneness. Bake for 15 minutes, or until done to your taste. Sprinkle with chopped parsley and serve with a croissant.

*Note: Chicken stock paste is available in small jars in the soup aisle of most groceries. You can substitute milk for the half & half for a lower fat dish, but it will take a little longer for the sauce to thicken.

1904 Secret Garden

E ven the locals are intrigued by the New Orleans-style front gate that takes you from Main Street right into the charmed atmosphere of the Secret Garden Bed & Breakfast. When you open the gate, you will be greeted by a serene and private setting created by the tall native hemlock hedges. You will be nestled secretly and comfortably in the mountain village atmosphere in Weaverville. Get ready to relax and be pampered!

The large, en-suite bedrooms are replete with fine linens, stylish furniture and soothing colors to provide an experience of comfortable elegance.

INNKEEPERS:	Cassandra Clark
ADDRESS:	56 North Main Street
	Weaverville, North Carolina 28787
TELEPHONE:	(828) 658-9317; (800) 797-8211
E-MAIL:	garden56@aol.com
WEBSITE:	www.secretgardennc.com
ROOMS:	3 Rooms; 3 Suites; Private baths
CHILDREN:	Children age 16 and older welcome
ANIMALS:	Not allowed
HANDICAPPED:	Not handicapped accessible
DIETARY NEEDS:	Will accommodate guests' special dietary needs

Pipérade with Poached Eggs

Makes 4 Servings

"A pipérade is a Basque dish of tomatoes and bell peppers cooked in olive oil with the chef's choice of additional ingredients. This is a very attractively colored dish. I serve it on Saturdays as a dish to 'get up and go' rather than a Sunday comfort dish." ~ Innkeeper, 1904 Secret Garden Bed & Breakfast

1	tablespoon extra-virgin olive oil
4	andouille sausages, cut diagonally into ½-inch-thick slices
1	yellow onion, thinly sliced
2	cloves garlic, thinly sliced
2	red bell peppers, cut into ¼-inch-thick slices
3	large tomatoes, peeled, seeded and diced
¼	teaspoon crushed red pepper flakes

Salt and black pepper, to taste

8	(½-inch-thick) slices country bread, toasted
8	eggs
2	tablespoons chopped parsley or chives, for garnish

Heat oil in a skillet over medium-high heat. Add sausage and cook for 5-7 minutes, stirring occasionally, until browned; remove to a plate with a slotted spoon. Drain excess grease from skillet.

Lower heat to medium. Add onion, garlic and bell pepper to skillet; cook for 8-10 minutes, until softened. Add sausage, tomatoes and red pepper flakes; cook for about 5 minutes, until liquid evaporates and tomatoes are soft. Season with salt and pepper. Poach eggs. Put 2 slices of toast on each plate. Spoon sausage mixture over toast. Top with a poached egg. Sprinkle eggs with parsley or chives to serve.

The Kerr House

The Kerr House, located in one of Statesville's three residential historic districts, was built in 1891. Statesville is conveniently located at the crossroads of Interstates 40 and 77. This exceptional access, along with the close proximity to Charlotte, Winston-Salem, Greensboro, Hickory and High Point (the furniture market capital of the United States), makes Statesville a perfect destination for a getaway.

If you are looking for great buys in the furniture market, you've come to the right place. Buy at a discount and have it shipped home!

INNKEEPERS:	Margaret & Edmond Pendrich
ADDRESS:	519 Davie Avenue
	Statesville, North Carolina 28677
TELEPHONE:	(704) 881-0957; (877) 308-0353
E-MAIL:	thekerrhouse@abts.net
WEBSITE:	www.statesville-nc-lodging.com
ROOMS:	4 Rooms; Private baths
CHILDREN:	Welcome
ANIMALS:	Not allowed
HANDICAPPED:	Not handicapped accessible
DIETARY NEEDS:	Will accommodate guests' special dietary needs

Goat Cheese & Apple Omelet

Makes 2 Servings

4   tablespoons butter, divided
2   apples, peeled and thinly sliced
1   tablespoon brown sugar
1   tablespoon amaretto or other almond liqueur
4   eggs
2   tablespoons half & half or cream
Salt and black pepper, to taste
2   ounces goat cheese, crumbled
Toast points, for serving

Melt 2 tablespoons of butter in a skillet over medium heat. Add apples and cook until just softened. Sprinkle apples with brown sugar and cook for a couple minutes longer, stirring to coat. Stir in amaretto, remove from heat and set aside.

Beat eggs and half & half. Season with salt and pepper. Melt 1 tablespoon of butter in each of 2 small omelet pans or skillets (or use a medium skillet and make 1 large omelet). Divide egg mixture between pans. When omelets are set, top each with ½ of apple mixture and ½ of goat cheese. Fold omelets in half and cook for 1 minute more. Serve immediately with toast points.

The Inn at Celebrity Dairy

The Inn at Celebrity Dairy welcomes you to the peace and comfort of an old home-place and the purposeful life of a 300-acre working dairy in rural Chatham County. A community gathering place for over a century, Celebrity Dairy now extends its warm welcome and informal comfort to guests year-round.

Wake refreshed to join the farm crew for a breakfast of (naturally) chèvre (goat cheese) omelets or home-baked pastries, along with seasonal fruits and preserves from the neighbor's gardens.

INNKEEPERS:	Brit Pfann & John Bonitz
ADDRESS:	144 Celebrity Dairy Way
	Siler City, North Carolina 27344
TELEPHONE:	(919) 742-5176; (877) 742-5176
E-MAIL:	theinn@celebritydairy.com
WEBSITE:	www.celebritydairy.com
ROOMS:	7 Rooms; 1 Suite; Private & shared baths
CHILDREN:	Welcome
ANIMALS:	Not allowed; Resident outdoor cats & farm animals
HANDICAPPED:	Handicapped accessible
DIETARY NEEDS:	Will accommodate guests' special dietary needs

Caramelized Onion & Goat Cheese Omelet

Makes 6 Servings

"We serve this rustic country omelet on a large platter with roasted potatoes. The omelette is good served cold or hot, or try slicing it into thin shreds and using it as a salad topping." - Innkeeper, Inn at Celebrity Dairy

4   tablespoons canola oil, divided
2   large onions, chopped
12   large eggs
2   tablespoons water or milk
4   ounces goat cheese, crumbled
Lemon pepper and black pepper, to taste
Fresh herbs, for garnish

Heat 2 tablespoons of oil in a skillet over medium-low heat. Add onions and cook until golden. Lower heat to low and cook, stirring occasionally, for 30-45 minutes, until well caramelized (golden brown and sweet).

In a bowl, beat eggs and water until frothy and light yellow. Heat remaining 2 tablespoons of oil in an omelet pan over medium heat until oil is almost smoking. Add eggs. As eggs cook, lift edges of omelet and let uncooked eggs flow underneath and come in contact with pan.

Lower heat to low and sprinkle caramelized onions and goat cheese over half of eggs. Season with lemon pepper and black pepper. Release eggs from pan (use a spatula, if needed) and fold uncovered half of eggs over onions and goat cheese. Cover and let stand at low heat or off the heat until eggs are set. Invert a serving plate over pan, then invert pan and turn omelet out onto plate, bottom-side-up. Garnish with fresh herbs and serve.

Corner Oak Manor

The Corner Oak Manor Bed & Breakfast is located in a 1920 English Tudor home, situated in a quiet neighborhood just a half mile from the historic Biltmore House. Come nurture your senses in this comfortably elegant home. Your hosts will make you feel welcome and pampered. At Corner Oak Manor, you'll find sumptuous gourmet breakfasts, a refreshing jacuzzi and gracious amenities in a relaxed ambiance.

If you want extra privacy, the cottage is the place for you! It has a living room/kitchen area with elaborately stenciled walls and a gas fireplace.

INNKEEPERS:	Karen & Andy Spradley
ADDRESS:	53 Saint Dunstans Road
	Asheville, North Carolina 28803
TELEPHONE:	(828) 253-3525; (888) 633-3525
E-MAIL:	info@corneroakmanor.com
WEBSITE:	www.corneroakmanor.com
ROOMS:	3 Rooms; 1 Cottage; Private baths
CHILDREN:	Children age 12 and older welcome
ANIMALS:	Not allowed
HANDICAPPED:	Not handicapped accessible
DIETARY NEEDS:	Will accommodate guests' special dietary needs

Smoked Trout Frittata

Makes 4 to 6 Servings

3   medium red potatoes
2   teaspoons extra-virgin olive oil
1   large onion, chopped
Salt and black pepper, to taste
6   large eggs
¼   cup milk
1   tablespoon prepared horseradish
1   tablespoon chopped fresh dill (or 1 teaspoon dried dill)
¾   cup flaked smoked trout (or flaked smoked salmon fillet)

Put potatoes in small saucepan with cold water to cover. Bring to a boil, lower heat and simmer just until tender; drain and cool potatoes. Slice potatoes in half lengthwise and then into ¼-inch-thick slices.

Preheat oven to 350°F. Heat olive oil in an oven-proof skillet over medium heat. Add onion and cook until soft. Add potatoes. Season with salt and pepper. Whisk together eggs, milk, salt, pepper, horseradish and dill; pour over ingredients in skillet. Top with smoked trout. Transfer skillet to oven and bake for 20 minutes, or until eggs are set. If desired, broil for 1-2 minutes to slightly brown top. Slice and serve hot or at room temperature.

The Yellow House

The Yellow House
Waynesville

Like a grand old duchess on a throne, the Yellow House on Plott Creek Road sits on top of a hill, looking out across the misty green of the Blue Ridge Mountains, across a pastoral kingdom with cows in the meadow and frogs in the lily pond.

Guest rooms borrow their colors from impressionist paintings and their playful serenity from the French countryside. And, all of the pleasures of the Blue Ridge Mountains are almost as close as your bedside breakfast!

INNKEEPERS:	Donna & Stephen Shea
ADDRESS:	89 Oakview Drive
	Waynesville, North Carolina 28786
TELEPHONE:	(828) 452-0991; (800) 563-1236
E-MAIL:	info@theyellowhouse.com
WEBSITE:	www.theyellowhouse.com
ROOMS:	10 Rooms; Private baths
CHILDREN:	Children age 12 and older welcome
ANIMALS:	Not allowed
HANDICAPPED:	Not handicapped accessible
DIETARY NEEDS:	Will accommodate guests' special dietary needs

Autumn Vegetable Frittata

Makes 6 Servings

"This frittata can be prepared the night before and baked in the morning. You can substitute any vegetables you would like, such as broccoli, green or red bell peppers, celery, etc. Don't be afraid to experiment – this is fairly foolproof." – Innkeeper, The Yellow House

3	links Italian sausage
1	tablespoon vegetable oil
2	small yellow squash, sliced
1	large zucchini, sliced
1	large carrot, sliced
1	medium onion, chopped
6	ounces fresh mushrooms, sliced
6	eggs
3	large cloves garlic, minced
1	cup grated Parmesan cheese
½	teaspoon dried basil
¼	teaspoon dried marjoram

Salt and black pepper, to taste

1 cup grated cheese (cheddar, Swiss or a mixture)

Preheat oven to 350°F. Remove sausages from casings and cook in a large skillet over medium heat, breaking up sausage into small pieces, until cooked through; drain on paper towels and set aside. Heat oil in a skillet over medium heat. Add squash, zucchini, carrots, onions and mushrooms; cook until vegetables are crisp-tender.

In a large bowl, beat eggs, garlic, Parmesan cheese, basil, marjoram, salt and pepper. Stir in sausage and squash mixture; pour mixture into a greased deep-dish pie pan or a 9x9-inch baking dish. Sprinkle with cheddar or Swiss cheese. Bake for 30 minutes (or cover and refrigerate overnight and bake the next day).

Note: This frittata freezes well after it is baked. Thaw it in the refrigerator, then heat it through in a preheated 300°F oven (do not overcook it).

Colby House

The circa 1924, AAA Three Diamond Colby House offers discriminating travelers an elegant retreat into years gone by with all the comforts of modern living and none of the pressures. Located in the heart of Asheville, in the Montford Historic District, the inn is within one mile of downtown shopping, dining and entertainment.

The Celebration Cottage boasts a cozy atmosphere with a parlor with fireplace, a kitchen and a whirlpool tub and separate shower. A patio in the shady English garden, just outside the door, is enhanced by a Koi fish pond.

INNKEEPERS:	Peter & Bonnie Marsh
ADDRESS:	230 Pearson Drive
	Asheville, North Carolina 28801
TELEPHONE:	(828) 253-5644; (800) 982-2118
E-MAIL:	colbyhouse@cs.com
WEBSITE:	www.colbyhouse.com
ROOMS:	4 Rooms; 1 Cottage; Private baths
CHILDREN:	Call ahead
ANIMALS:	Not allowed
HANDICAPPED:	Not handicapped accessible
DIETARY NEEDS:	Will accommodate guests' special dietary needs

Florentine Frittata

Makes 6 Servings

12   eggs
¾   cup ricotta cheese
2   teaspoons plus 2⅓ tablespoons vegetable oil
Salt and black pepper, to taste
¾   cup sliced mushrooms
1   large clove garlic, minced
4   green onions, sliced
1   teaspoon mixed dried herbs (such as basil, thyme, oregano, etc.)
4   cups coarsely chopped fresh spinach
1   red bell pepper, diced
½   cup grated cheddar cheese
½   cup grated mozzarella cheese

Preheat broiler. In a bowl, combine eggs, ricotta cheese, 2 teaspoons of oil, salt and pepper. Heat the 2⅓ tablespoons of oil in a large cast-iron skillet or other oven-proof skillet over medium heat. Add mushrooms, garlic and green onions; cook for 2 minutes. Add herbs, spinach and bell pepper; cook for 2 minutes. Remove skillet from heat and spread vegetable mixture over bottom of skillet.

Sprinkle cheddar cheese over ingredients in skillet. Pour egg mixture over cheese. Return skillet to heat and cook, stirring, until eggs are half-cooked, then sprinkle with mozzarella cheese. Transfer skillet to oven and broil until eggs are set and cheese is bubbly. Cut into wedges and serve.

C.W. Worth House

The C.W. Worth House is located in Wilmington, one of the most beautiful cities on the Carolina coast. Founded over 250 years ago, on the shores of the Cape Fear River, Wilmington has a gracious past. The historic district is the largest one listed in the National Register of Historic Places and is a must see. Many fascinating buildings and historic sites are open to the visitor, so you can easily spend a few days exploring.

Browse the many quaint shops in the historic district or take a "Southern-style stroll" down brick streets rich in architecture.

INNKEEPERS:	Margi & Doug Erickson
ADDRESS:	412 South Third Street
	Wilmington, North Carolina 28401
TELEPHONE:	(910) 763-2173; (800) 340-8559
E-MAIL:	info@worthhouse.com
WEBSITE:	www.worthhouse.com
ROOMS:	7 Rooms; Private baths
CHILDREN:	Children age 12 and older welcome
ANIMALS:	Not allowed; Resident cat
HANDICAPPED:	Not handicapped accessible
DIETARY NEEDS:	Will accommodate guests' special dietary needs

Rosemary & Goat Cheese Strata

Makes 8 Servings

"We serve this strata with bacon and a broiled tomato." ~ Innkeeper, C.W. Worth House Bed & Breakfast

1   loaf rustic bread, such as Ciabatta, sliced and torn into 1-inch pieces
8-10 sprigs fresh rosemary plus extra, for garnish
6-8   ounces goat or feta cheese or a combination, to your taste
12   large eggs
3½   cups half & half or milk
¼   teaspoon cayenne
¼-½   teaspoon dried thyme
Crème fraîche*
Paprika, for garnish

Preheat oven to 350°F. Butter 8 (4-ounce) ramekins. Put bread in a large bowl. Chop rosemary leaves and sprinkle over bread. Crumble in goat or feta cheese and mix gently with a slotted spoon.

In a bowl, whisk together eggs, half & half, cayenne and dried thyme. Pour egg mixture over bread and mix gently with a large slotted spoon until well combined. Divide bread mixture among ramekins, filling each ¾-full.

Put ramekins on a baking sheet. Bake for 25-35 minutes, until puffed and golden. Remove from oven and let stand for 5 minutes. With a flexible spatula, remove stratas to plates. Drizzle crème fraîche over stratas. Sprinkle with a little paprika and top with a sprig of fresh rosemary to serve.

*Note: If you cannot find crème fraîche, substitute sour cream thinned to a drizzling consistency with a little whipping cream or half & half.

1889 WhiteGate Inn & Cottage

The five distinctive guest rooms in the 1889 WhiteGate Inn each honor a distinguished American poet. The rooms are uniquely decorated, reflecting different period styles including English, Arts and Crafts and Victorian. Poetry volumes by the featured poets are included in each room.

The WhiteGate Cottage was built in 1889 as part of the original estate. The cottage provides a secluded, romantic haven with a two-person Jacuzzi tub, separate large shower and gas-log fireplaces in the living room and bedroom. It also has a porch to enjoy the beautiful evening view.

INNKEEPERS:	Ralph Coffey & Frank Salvo
ADDRESS:	173 East Chestnut Street
	Asheville, North Carolina 28801
TELEPHONE:	(828) 253-2553; (800) 485-3045
E-MAIL:	innkeeper@whitegate.net
WEBSITE:	www.whitegate.net
ROOMS:	2 Rooms; 3 Suites; 1 Cottage; Private baths
CHILDREN:	Children age 15 and older welcome
ANIMALS:	Not allowed
HANDICAPPED:	Not handicapped accessible
DIETARY NEEDS:	Will accommodate guests' special dietary needs

Bacon & Potato Strata

Makes 8 to 12 Servings

This strata may be prepared the night before, covered, refrigerated and baked in the morning.

3	tablespoons vegetable oil
½	(26-ounce) package frozen hash brown potatoes
1	(3-ounce) package Ready Crisp bacon bits or 3 ounces bacon, cooked and crumbled
8	slices Canadian bacon, diced
8	ounces mushrooms, sliced
1	leek, chopped
16	eggs
1½	cups milk
½	teaspoon salt
½	teaspoon dried rosemary
¼	teaspoon dried thyme
2	cups grated mozzarella cheese

Preheat oven to 350°F. Grease a 9x13-inch baking dish. Heat oil in a skillet over medium-high heat. Add hash browns and cook until soft. Layer hash browns, bacon bits, Canadian bacon, mushrooms, leeks and cheese in baking dish.

Beat eggs, milk, salt, rosemary, thyme and cheese; pour over ingredients in baking dish. Bake for 1 hour, or until golden brown. Remove from oven and let stand for 5 minutes, then slice and serve.

C.W. Worth House

Charles W. Worth, a wholesale grocery merchant and a commission merchant in cotton and naval stores, purchased this property in 1889. He had the existing home demolished and began construction of this Queen Anne-style home in 1889. It was completed in 1893 and the Worth family resided in the home until 1930. The house became an inn in 1985.

The C.W. Worth House's breakfast offers hearty fare to start the day and includes entrées such as savory rosemary and goat cheese bread pudding, artichoke and mushroom quiche or banana oat pancakes.

INNKEEPERS:	**Margi & Doug Erickson**
ADDRESS:	412 South Third Street
	Wilmington, North Carolina 28401
TELEPHONE:	(910) 763-2173; (800) 340-8559
E-MAIL:	info@worthhouse.com
WEBSITE:	www.worthhouse.com
ROOMS:	7 Rooms; Private baths
CHILDREN:	Children age 12 and older welcome
ANIMALS:	Not allowed; Resident cat
HANDICAPPED:	Not handicapped accessible
DIETARY NEEDS:	Will accommodate guests' special dietary needs

Spinach & Cheese Croissant Strata

Makes 8 Servings

8   large croissants, torn into bite-size pieces
2   cups grated Monterey Jack or Swiss cheese, divided
1   (10-ounce) package frozen spinach, thawed and squeezed dry
8   large eggs
2   cups milk
Hot sauce, to taste
Worcestershire sauce, to taste
1   teaspoon chopped fresh herbs, such as basil, rosemary, sage, marjoram, etc.

Preheat oven to 350°F. Layer croissant pieces in a lightly greased 9x13-inch baking pan. Sprinkle with 1 cup of cheese. Top with spinach. Beat eggs, milk, remaining 1 cup of cheese, hot sauce, Worcestershire and herbs; pour over ingredients in baking pan.

Cover pan loosely with foil sprayed with non-stick cooking spray and bake for 15 minutes. Remove foil and rotate pan for more even baking. Bake for 30 minutes more (check occasionally and cover with foil if top is browning too quickly), until a knife inserted in center comes out clean. Remove from oven and let stand for 5 minutes. Slice into 8 pieces and serve.

Chateau on the Mountain

Chateau
Bed & Breakfast — ON THE MOUNTAIN

Perched high atop Hoopers Creek Valley, the Chateau on the Mountain combines old-world charm and elegance with modern conveniences and amenities. The Chateau's mission is to pamper guests with every luxury and service so that their inn experience will always exceed expectations.

Surrounded by thousands of acres of mountains and meadows, the inn is situated on over ten acres of beautiful lawns and forested lumber trails with magnificent views. Explore the area on your own or join the innkeepers for a group trek.

INNKEEPERS:	Jeanne & Lee Yudin
ADDRESS:	1048 Sandy Flat Mountain Road
	Fletcher, North Carolina 28732
TELEPHONE:	(828) 651-9810; (888) 591-6281
E-MAIL:	innkeepers@chateauonthemountain.com
WEBSITE:	www.chateauonthemountain.com
ROOMS:	3 Rooms; 3 Suites; Private baths
CHILDREN:	Welcome
ANIMALS:	Not allowed
HANDICAPPED:	Handicapped accessible
DIETARY NEEDS:	Will accommodate guests' special dietary needs

Chateau Quiche Asparagus

Makes 6 Servings

"My husband does all the cooking (we kid about 'do I know where the kitchen is'). So when my husband had to go out of town and I was tossed into the fray, I panicked. I had not cooked breakfast for a large group of people in a long time, so I fell back on a recipe that I used to make for brunch. Our guests said it was the best quiche they had ever had."~ Innkeeper, Chateau on the Mountain

1	deep-dish frozen pie crust
⅓	pound Swiss cheese, grated
¾	pound bacon, cooked and chopped or crumbled plus extra, for garnish
4	eggs
1½	cups milk
2	tablespoons butter, melted
1	tablespoon all-purpose flour

Dash of salt
⅛	teaspoon nutmeg plus extra, for garnish
5	stalks asparagus, washed and bottoms trimmed plus extra, for garnish

Preheat oven to 350°F. Sprinkle cheese and bacon in alternating layers in crust. Beat eggs, milk and butter. Put flour, salt and nutmeg in a small cup and add a very small amount of egg mixture; stir until a smooth paste is formed. Add a little more egg mixture and stir until a thin paste is formed (this will prevent lumps). Add flour mixture to egg mixture; mix well and pour over ingredients in crust.

Cut asparagus stalks to about half the diameter of the crust (about ½ stalk). Arrange stalks in a spoke-like fashion on top of ingredients in crust. Bake for 40 minutes, or until set (quiche will seem a little loose when removed from oven). Top with crumbled bacon and a little nutmeg. Let stand for 5 minutes, then slice and serve on plates decorated with raw or slightly cooked asparagus.

The Kerr House

The circa 1891 Kerr House is set in one of Statesville's three residential historic districts. The area has many beautiful homes of later Victorian design on wide, tree-shaded streets. The comfortable atmosphere of earlier years has been retained to a large degree, providing a beautiful setting for a walk. Few intrusions mark the district's appearance with 85 percent of the buildings constructed prior to 1930.

Statesville's commercial historic district and its residential historic districts are all listed in the National Register of Historic Places.

INNKEEPERS:	Margaret & Edmond Pendrich
ADDRESS:	519 Davie Avenue
	Statesville, North Carolina 28677
TELEPHONE:	(704) 881-0957; (877) 308-0353
E-MAIL:	thekerrhouse@abts.net
WEBSITE:	www.statesville-nc-lodging.com
ROOMS:	4 Rooms; Private baths
CHILDREN:	Welcome
ANIMALS:	Not allowed
HANDICAPPED:	Not handicapped accessible
DIETARY NEEDS:	Will accommodate guests' special dietary needs

Savory Cheesecake

Makes 8 to 10 Servings

3   (8-ounce) packages cream cheese, softened
5   eggs
2   tablespoons half & half
Crushed red pepper flakes, to taste (optional)
1¼ cups grated cheddar cheese
1   pound bulk sage sausage, cooked and drained
1   (9-inch) pie crust

Preheat oven to 375°F. In a bowl, with a mixer, whip cream cheese. Beat in eggs, 1 at a time, scraping down sides of bowl after each addition. Add half & half, red pepper flakes and cheddar cheese; mix thoroughly. Stir in sausage. Pour cream cheese mixture into crust and bake for 1 hour.

Note: This cheesecake freezes well. You can add any ingredients you like to the basic recipe, such as cooked diced onion, sliced mushrooms or crumbled bacon or minced fresh herbs.

C.W. Worth House

The distinctive dual turrets of the C.W. Worth House represent one of Wilmington's most charming bed & breakfasts. Decorated with fanciful shingles, this inn is a Queen Anne confection offering seven well-appointed guestrooms. As you step through the gate, the spacious Southern porch invites you to slow down, relax and enjoy.

A visit to a historic bed & breakfast inn is a special event in itself. It is reminiscent of days gone by and a past rich in history. The experience lets you share past Southern traditions in a rather extraordinary fashion.

INNKEEPERS:	Margi & Doug Erickson
ADDRESS:	412 South Third Street
	Wilmington, North Carolina 28401
TELEPHONE:	(910) 763-2173; (800) 340-8559
E-MAIL:	info@worthhouse.com
WEBSITE:	www.worthhouse.com
ROOMS:	7 Rooms; Private baths
CHILDREN:	Children age 12 and older welcome
ANIMALS:	Not allowed; Resident cat
HANDICAPPED:	Not handicapped accessible
DIETARY NEEDS:	Will accommodate guests' special dietary needs

Artichoke Mushroom Flan

Makes 6 Servings

"We serve this flan with bacon or sausage and a broiled tomato." ~ Innkeeper, C.W. Worth House Bed & Breakfast

Dough for 1 pie crust

1	(14½-ounce) can whole artichoke hearts (not marinated)
1	(10-ounce) can sliced mushrooms
1	cup grated Swiss cheese
3	eggs plus 2 egg whites
1	cup whipping cream
½	teaspoon dried thyme plus fresh thyme sprigs, for garnish
¼	teaspoon cayenne pepper, or to taste
1	teaspoon dry mustard

Preheat oven to 350°F. Line a 10-inch glass pie pan with pie crust. Drain artichokes, squeeze out liquid and roughly chop; spread over crust. Drain and roughly chop mushrooms; spread over artichokes. Sprinkle with cheese.

Beat eggs and egg whites. Add cream, dried thyme, cayenne and mustard; mix well and pour over ingredients in crust. Bake for 40-50 minutes, until risen and nicely browned, and a knife inserted in center comes out clean. Remove from oven. Let stand for 5 minutes. Slice and serve garnished with thyme sprigs.

1902 Turnpike House

In 1902, Thomas Lowe and his bride, Bettie Banner, built this home which became a welcoming gathering place for family and friends. Today, spend happy hours overlooking the secluded, tranquil grounds from rocking chairs or the swing on the expansive front porch.

On cooler evenings, retreat to the elegant but comfortable gathering room around the slate hearth and wood-burning stove. Later, retire to your private quarters, a cozy oasis beautifully appointed with an eclectic blend of antiques, art and family treasures.

INNKEEPERS:	Paul & Cindy Goedhart
ADDRESS:	317 Old Turnpike Road
	Banner Elk, North Carolina 28604
TELEPHONE:	(828) 898-5611; (888) 802-4487
E-MAIL:	info@1902turnpikehouse.com
WEBSITE:	www.1902turnpikehouse.com
ROOMS:	7 Rooms; Private baths
CHILDREN:	Children age 10 and older welcome
ANIMALS:	Not allowed; Resident dog
HANDICAPPED:	Not handicapped accessible
DIETARY NEEDS:	Will accommodate guests' special dietary needs

Turnpike House Egg Casserole

Makes 6 to 12 Servings

"This is our most requested recipe. It is prepared the night before and baked in the morning. It also can be cooked, frozen and reheated or be halved and baked in a 9x9-inch pan." - Innkeeper, Turnpike House Bed & Breakfast

1	pound bacon, chopped
2-3	tablespoons butter or margarine
2	small onions, chopped
1¼	pounds mushrooms, sliced
2	cups cooked wild rice
1½	cups grated Swiss cheese
¾	cup grated Monterey Jack cheese
1	cup herb seasoned stuffing mix
½	cup chopped parsley
½	teaspoon nutmeg
1	teaspoon salt
½	teaspoon black pepper
18	eggs
2½	cups cream or half & half
2	(10¾-ounce) cans cream of mushroom soup
1	(10¾-ounce) can cheddar cheese soup

Cook bacon until crisp. Drain and cool bacon, reserving bacon drippings. Use some of the bacon drippings to grease a 9x13-inch baking dish. Heat 2 tablespoons of bacon drippings in a skillet over medium heat. Add butter and onions; cook until onions are soft. Add mushrooms and cook until tender and most of liquid has evaporated; set aside and cool.

In a large bowl, combine bacon, mushroom mixture, wild rice, Swiss and Monterey Jack cheeses, stuffing, parsley, nutmeg, salt and pepper. In a medium bowl, mix eggs and cream; pour over rice mixture and stir to combine. Pour mixture into baking dish, cover and refrigerate overnight.

The next morning, bring casserole to room temperature. Preheat oven to 350°F. Bake for 50 minutes. Serve with a sauce made by combining and heating mushroom and cheddar cheese soups (diluted with water, if desired).

Thomas Walton Manor

Larry Horne, Thomas Walton Manor's owner, is a Laurinburg native. As a child, he would pass the house and wonder at its beauty, longing to slip beyond the iron gate, climb the winding staircase and explore the 15 rooms. However, it was some 30 years and a career as a world-renown interior designer in the Washington, D.C. area before his dream came true.

Mr. Horne has filled the house with color, hand-painted murals, stenciled floors, marble bathrooms, Italian chandeliers and rich fabrics. He blends old and new, making each room a distinctive, yet tranquil experience.

INNKEEPERS:	Ron Phillips, Larry Horne & Anne Moberg
ADDRESS:	400 West Church Street
	Laurinburg, North Carolina 28352
TELEPHONE:	(910) 276-0551
E-MAIL:	relax@thomaswaltonmanor.com
WEBSITE:	www.thomaswaltonmanor.com
ROOMS:	2 Rooms; 3 Suites; 1 Apartment; Private baths
CHILDREN:	Children age 14 and older welcome
ANIMALS:	Small dogs welcome in apartment
HANDICAPPED:	Not handicapped accessible
DIETARY NEEDS:	Will accommodate guests' special dietary needs

Egg Casserole with Herbs

Makes 6 Servings

"This casserole is delicious for brunch or lunch. When serving at lunch, my aunt, who gave me this recipe, included raspberry Jell-o with fresh raspberries, served in a cut glass bowl, assorted cookies and spiced tea." ~ Innkeeper, Thomas Walton Manor

12	hard-boiled eggs, sliced
2	(10½-ounce) cans cream of mushroom or cream of celery soup
1	cup milk
1	cup sour cream
½	cup grated cheddar cheese
¼	cup chopped pimentos
1	tablespoon snipped fresh chives
1½	teaspoons chopped fresh thyme or ½ teaspoon dried thyme
12	slices bacon, cooked crisp and crumbled

Paprika, for garnish

6	English muffins, split and toasted

Fresh parsley sprigs, for garnish

Preheat oven to 350°F. Layer eggs in a buttered 9x13-inch baking dish. In a bowl, combine soup, milk, sour cream, cheese, pimentos, chives and thyme; pour over eggs. Bake for 20 minutes. Remove casserole from oven and sprinkle with bacon and paprika. Bake for 10 minutes more, then remove from oven and let stand for 5 minutes. Serve over toasted English muffins and garnish with parsley.

Meadows Inn

B uilt in 1980 as weekend lodging for visitors coming to see the Tryon Palace, the Meadows Inn has since grown to offer year-round lodging.

"The Tryon Palace was built between 1767 and 1770, as the first capitol of the colony of North Carolina and a home for the royal governor and his family. Josiah Martin, the second royal governor to live in the Palace, fled in 1775 at the start of the American Revolution. Patriots made the Palace their capitol and the first sessions of the general assembly met there to begin designing a free and independent state." ~ Tyron Palace

INNKEEPERS:	John & Betty Foy
ADDRESS:	212 Pollock Street
	New Bern, North Carolina 28560
TELEPHONE:	(252) 634-1776; (877) 551-1776
E-MAIL:	meadowsinnbnb@earthlink.net
WEBSITE:	www.meadowsinn-nc.com
ROOMS:	6 Rooms; 1 Suite; Private baths
CHILDREN:	Welcome
ANIMALS:	Not allowed
HANDICAPPED:	Not handicapped accessible
DIETARY NEEDS:	Will accommodate guests' special dietary needs

Meadows Inn Breakfast Casserole

Makes 10 to 12 Servings

"Plan ahead, this casserole needs to be started the night before." - Innkeeper, Meadows Inn Bed & Breakfast

1	pound bulk country sausage
8	eggs
1	(10-ounce) package frozen cut asparagus, thawed and drained
10	cups cubed bread (from about 10 slices of bread)
3	cups milk
2	tablespoons all-purpose flour
1	tablespoon dry mustard
2	cups sliced fresh mushrooms (about 8 ounces of mushrooms)
2	teaspoons basil
1	teaspoon salt

Black pepper, to taste

2	tablespoons butter or margarine, melted
1	cup grated sharp cheddar or Swiss cheese (optional)

Brown sausage in a skillet over medium heat; drain. In a large bowl, beat eggs. Add asparagus, bread, sausage, milk, flour, mustard, mushrooms, basil, salt and pepper; mix well. Grease a 9x13-inch baking pan. Pour melted butter into pan and rotate pan to coat with butter. Pour egg mixture over butter. Cover and refrigerate overnight.

The next day, preheat oven to 350°F. Uncover casserole and sprinkle with cheese, if desired. Bake for 60-70 minutes, until a knife inserted in center comes out clean.

Morehead Manor

B uilt in 1910 for the CEO of Liggett and Meyers, this splendidly
decorated 8,000-square-foot, Colonial Revival-style home is located
within walking distance of downtown, the Durham Bulls Ballpark and
historic Brightleaf Square.

A place where elegance, excitement and hospitality meet, guests can spend
the afternoon listening to music, having tea or enjoying a good book in any
of the inn's common areas. A full breakfast, complimentary beverages and
scrumptious homemade desserts are offered each day.

INNKEEPERS:	Daniel & Monica Edwards
ADDRESS:	914 Vickers Avenue
	Durham, North Carolina 27701
TELEPHONE:	(919) 687-4366; (888) 437-6333
E-MAIL:	info@moreheadmanor.com
WEBSITE:	www.moreheadmanor.com
ROOMS:	3 Rooms; 1 Suite; Private baths
CHILDREN:	Children age 12 and older welcome
ANIMALS:	Not allowed; Resident cat
HANDICAPPED:	Not handicapped accessible
DIETARY NEEDS:	Will accommodate guests' special dietary needs

Mom's Seafood Casserole

Makes 6 to 8 Servings

*"A childhood favorite that I have been able to pass on for my guests to enjoy." ~
Innkeeper, Morehead Manor Bed & Breakfast*

½   stick butter, melted
1   cup chopped onion
1   medium green bell pepper, chopped
½   cup chopped celery
½   cup wild rice, cooked according to package directions
½   cup white rice, cooked according to package directions
1   pound shrimp, cooked
6   ounces crabmeat with juice
2   (10¾-ounce) cans cream of mushroom soup
¼   cup water
1   (4-ounce) can sliced mushrooms, drained
1   (2-ounce) jar pimentos, drained
1   cup Pepperidge Farm stuffing mix

Preheat oven to 350°F. Grease a 9x13-inch baking dish. Melt butter in a
large skillet over medium heat. Add onion, bell pepper and celery; cook
until soft. Add remaining ingredients, except stuffing, and stir to combine;
put mixture in baking dish. Sprinkle with stuffing. Bake for 1 hour.

Lois Jane's Riverview Inn

Traditional Southern hospitality with a Southport flavor is yours to enjoy at Lois Jane's. The inn is just across the street from the river, and Southport's popular antique shops are a block away. Enjoy the gentle view of ships and sailboats from the veranda as you relax in the rocking chairs.

Located in the heart of Southport, this historic home was built in the 1890s by Lois Jane's grandfather. The house was restored by her children in 1995 and furnished with period furniture and accessories, many of them family heirlooms.

INNKEEPERS:	Carolyn Davis
ADDRESS:	106 West Bay Street
	Southport, North Carolina 28461
TELEPHONE:	(910) 457-6701
E-MAIL:	frontdesk@loisjanes.com
WEBSITE:	www.loisjanes.com
ROOMS:	4 Rooms; 1 Suite; Private & shared baths
CHILDREN:	Children age 12 and older welcome
ANIMALS:	Not allowed
HANDICAPPED:	Not handicapped accessible
DIETARY NEEDS:	Will accommodate guests' special dietary needs

Sausage & Egg Casserole

Makes 10 to 12 Servings

"Quick, easy, delicious – just right for any morning." ~ Innkeeper, Lois Jane's Riverview Inn

1   **pound bulk country sage sausage**
6   **slices white bread, crusts removed**
10   **large eggs**
1   **cup milk**
1   **cup grated mild cheddar cheese**
Salt and black pepper, to taste

Preheat oven to 350°F. Crumble sausage into a skillet over medium heat and cook until browned. Put bread in a 9x13-inch baking dish. Sprinkle sausage over bread. Beat eggs, milk, cheese, salt and pepper; pour over sausage. Bake for about 30 minutes, until casserole is bubbling and cheese is melted.

1900 Inn on Montford

The 1900 Inn on Montford invites you to discover bed & breakfast comfort and hospitality with a warmth and graciousness reminiscent of the Biltmore's Gilded Age. The inn has been lovingly and thoughtfully restored to create the inviting ambience of past splendor and elegance.

Located in the heart of the Montford Historic District, the inn exemplifies the Arts and Crafts style made popular in Asheville by noted society architect Richard Sharp Smith, supervising architect to Biltmore House. This house is considered to be one of his finest residential commissions.

INNKEEPERS:	Ron & Lynn Carlson
ADDRESS:	296 Montford
	Asheville, North Carolina 28801
TELEPHONE:	(828) 254-9569; (800) 254-9569
E-MAIL:	info@innonmontford.com
WEBSITE:	www.innonmontford.com
ROOMS:	4 Rooms; 1 Suite; Private baths
CHILDREN:	Children age 12 and older welcome
ANIMALS:	Not allowed; Resident cat
HANDICAPPED:	Not handicapped accessible
DIETARY NEEDS:	Will accommodate guests' special dietary needs

Brunch Enchiladas

Makes 6 Servings

Plan ahead, these enchiladas need to be refrigerated for 8 hours or overnight.

1   tablespoon vegetable oil
1   cup finely diced cooked ham, such as John Morrell
¼   cup sliced green onion
¼   cup finely chopped red bell pepper
¼   cup finely chopped green bell pepper
6   flour tortillas
1¼   cups grated sharp cheddar cheese, divided
2   large eggs
2   cups half & half
1½   teaspoons all-purpose flour
⅛   teaspoon garlic powder
1-2   drops hot pepper sauce
Salsa, for serving
Sour cream, for serving

Grease a 7x11-inch baking dish (or use individual oven-proof dishes). Heat oil in a skillet over medium heat. Add ham, green onion and red and green bell peppers; cook until vegetables are tender.

Put ¼ cup of vegetable mixture down center of each tortilla. Sprinkle with 3 tablespoons of cheese. Roll up each tortilla and place seam-side-down in baking dish.

In a bowl, beat eggs. Add half & half, flour, garlic powder and hot pepper sauce; mix well, then pour over tortillas. Cover and refrigerate for 8 hours or overnight.

Remove enchiladas from refrigerator 30 minutes before baking. Preheat oven to 350°F. Bake for 35-40 minutes, or until a knife inserted in center comes out clean. Sprinkle with remaining cheese during the last 5 minutes of baking time. Serve with salsa and sour cream.

Breakfast Side Dishes

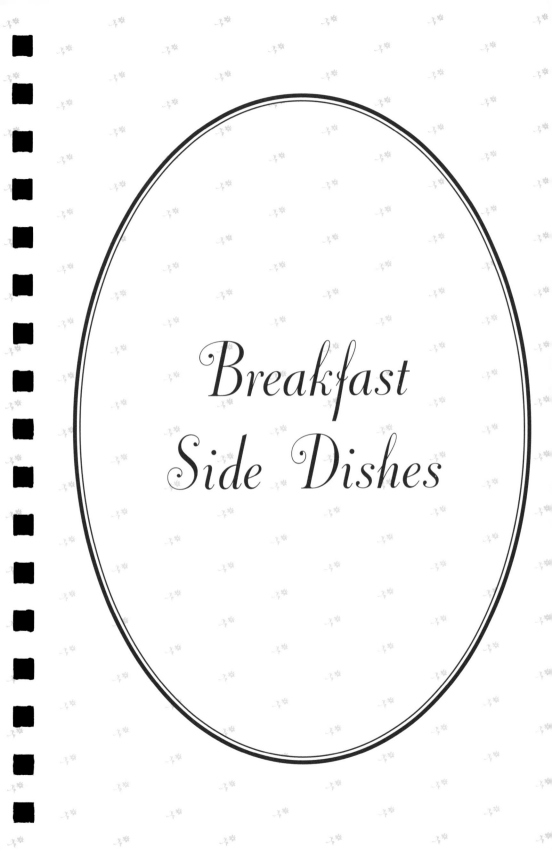

Breakfast
Side Dishes

Colonial Pines Inn

When you stay at the Colonial Pines Inn, you will experience the best Highlands has to offer. This exquisite and spacious year-round inn is located in town and is within walking distance of restaurants, boutiques, swimming, tennis and in-town natural attractions such as Sunset Rocks, Ravenel Lake and the Nature Center.

Rock on the veranda or stroll two acres of lawns dotted with hemlock, oak, maple and giant rhododendron. Sample currants, raspberries and blueberries from the garden before they find their way into the innkeepers' recipes!

INNKEEPERS:	Chris & Donna Alley
ADDRESS:	541 Hickory Street
	Highlands, North Carolina 28741
TELEPHONE:	(828) 526-2060
E-MAIL:	sleeptight@colonialpinesinn.com
WEBSITE:	www.colonialpinesinn.com
ROOMS:	3 Rooms; 3 Suites; 2 Cottages; Private baths
CHILDREN:	Call ahead
ANIMALS:	Not allowed
HANDICAPPED:	Not handicapped accessible
DIETARY NEEDS:	Will accommodate guests' special dietary needs

Potato Bacon Casserole

Makes 6 Servings

"A dish the whole family will enjoy. It can be prepared the night before, covered, refrigerated and then baked in the morning." ~ Innkeeper, Colonial Pines Inn

1½	cups grated extra-sharp cheddar cheese
½	(24-ounce) package frozen country-style hash browns
12	eggs
½	teaspoon salt
½	teaspoon black pepper
⅛	teaspoon cayenne pepper
2½	cups whole milk
1	pound bacon, cooked and crumbled
2	large green onions, chopped

Preheat oven to 325°F. Sprinkle ½ of cheese in a greased 9x13-inch baking dish. Sprinkle with ½ of hash browns. Repeat cheese and hash brown layers. In a bowl, beat eggs, salt, pepper and cayenne. Whisk in milk. Pour egg mixture over ingredients in baking dish. Top with bacon and green onions. Bake for 1 hour, then broil lightly to brown top.

Tip: Try "scrambling" the bacon in a skillet over medium heat, clipping it with scissors as it cooks. It doesn't need as much watching this way and you can assemble the rest of the ingredients while it is cooking.

The Duke Mansion

There is a long tradition of unforgettable hospitality at The Duke Mansion. Today the inn is dedicated to fine cuisine, remarkable service and beautiful presentation. With an emphasis on Southern charm in the Charlotte tradition, the chefs know how to add just the right flourish to make dining memorable.

Breakfast entrées may include banana pancakes with cranberry butter and maple syrup, eggs Benedict, smoked salmon and spinach quiche, shrimp and grits or coconut waffles with fruit compote and whipped cream.

INNKEEPERS:	The Lynnwood Foundation
ADDRESS:	400 Hermitage Road
	Charlotte, North Carolina 28207
TELEPHONE:	(704) 714-4400; (888) 202-1009
E-MAIL:	frontdesk@tlwf.com
WEBSITE:	www.dukemansion.org
ROOMS:	20 Rooms; Private baths
CHILDREN:	Welcome
ANIMALS:	Not allowed; Resident cats
HANDICAPPED:	Handicapped accessible
DIETARY NEEDS:	Will accommodate guests' special dietary needs

Sweet Potato, Artichoke & Crawfish Hash

Makes 4 Servings

Serve with Pan-Fried North Carolina Brook Trout (see recipe on page 209).

½	cup olive oil, divided
½	cup diced onion
¼	cup diced red bell pepper
¼	cup diced yellow bell pepper
¼	cup diced green bell pepper
1	pound sweet potatoes, diced
1	tablespoon minced garlic
4	ounces cooked crawfish tails, diced
½	cup marinated artichoke heart quarters
¼	cup chopped cilantro
¼	cup chopped parsley

Salt and black pepper, to taste

Heat ¼ cup of olive oil in a skillet over medium heat. Add onions and red, yellow and green bell peppers; cook until onions are translucent, then remove from heat and set aside to cool.

Heat remaining ¼ cup of olive oil in a skillet over medium heat. Add sweet potatoes and cook until tender and caramelized. Add onion mixture, garlic, crawfish, artichokes, cilantro and parsley. Season with salt and pepper. Heat through and serve.

The Moss House

L ocated one block from the Pamlico River and steeped in family history, the Moss House is a beautiful 1902 Victorian that provides gracious accommodations in the heart of historic downtown Washington. A short walk leads to a sailboat marina, shops, galleries, restaurants and a wonderful café for coffee and dessert. The Moss House is also at the start of the city's self-guided historic walking tour.

The Moss House offers a full breakfast highlighted by traditional Southern favorites that will prepare you for a full day of business or leisure pursuits.

INNKEEPERS:	Mary Havens Cooper
ADDRESS:	129 Van Norden Street
	Washington, North Carolina 27889
TELEPHONE:	(252) 975-3967
E-MAIL:	info@themosshouse.com
WEBSITE:	www.themosshouse.com
ROOMS:	4 Rooms; 1 Suite; Private baths
CHILDREN:	Children age 6 and older welcome
ANIMALS:	Not allowed; Resident cat in owner's quarters
HANDICAPPED:	Not handicapped accessible
DIETARY NEEDS:	Will accommodate guests' special dietary needs

Hashbrown Bake

Makes 6 to 8 Servings

"The recipe is adapted from the cookbook From Grandma's Kitchen. *It makes a perfect side dish for Sunday brunch or a potluck supper." ~ Innkeeper, The Moss House Bed & Breakfast*

1   (32-ounce) package frozen shredded hash browns
Salt and black pepper, to taste
½   cup chopped onion
1   cup sour cream
1   (10¾-ounce) can cream of chicken soup
3   cups grated cheddar cheese
1   stick butter, cut into pieces

Preheat oven to 350°F. Spread hash browns in a greased 9x13-inch baking pan. Season with salt and pepper. Combine onion, sour cream and soup; pour over potatoes. Sprinkle with cheese, then dot with butter. Bake for 60 minutes, or until top is golden.

Flint Street Inns

The Flint Street Inns offer the best in bed & breakfast accommodations, an authentic turn-of-the-century setting and a very convenient location for exploring the wonderful mountain community of Asheville. From this lovely, historic inn, you can easily stroll to downtown shops, galleries and restaurants.

Breakfast is a delight. There is always a daily inn specialty, which might be orange cinnamon French toast with apple cheddar sausage balls or vegetable and egg casserole with candied apples and baked ham.

INNKEEPERS:	Rick, Lynne & Marion Vogel
ADDRESS:	116 Flint Street
	Asheville, North Carolina 28801
TELEPHONE:	(828) 253-6723; (800) 234-8172
E-MAIL:	flintstreetinns@cs.com
WEBSITE:	www.flintstreetinns.com
ROOMS:	8 Rooms; Private baths
CHILDREN:	Children age 14 and older welcome
ANIMALS:	Not allowed
HANDICAPPED:	Not handicapped accessible
DIETARY NEEDS:	Will accommodate guests' special dietary needs

Apple Cheddar Sausage Balls

Makes 12 Sausage Balls

"We serve these with our orange-cinnamon French toast." ~ Innkeeper, Flint Street Inns

1   pound bulk sausage
1   cup grated sharp cheddar cheese
1   egg
½   cup unseasoned bread crumbs (or make your own with 4 slices of toasted bread)
2   small apples (unpeeled), cored and cut into bite-size pieces

Preheat oven to 300°F. Mix all ingredients. Using an ice cream scoop, form mixture into 2-inch balls. Put sausage balls on a greased rimmed baking sheet and bake for 30-45 minutes, until done.

Note: This recipe can be prepared ahead and frozen. To freeze, put baked sausage balls on a baking sheet pan and partially freeze them, then seal in a freezer bag, store in the freezer and reheat as needed.

The Trott House Inn

L ocated in Newton, the county seat of Catawba County, the Trott House Inn gives guests a chance to enjoy such local attractions as the Blue Ridge Parkway and the Hickory Furniture Mart and Hickory Antiques Mall with over 100 retailers and beautiful antiques and collectible Barbies. In winter, there is skiing only one hour away in the bordering mountains.

After a busy day, return to the inn and pamper yourself with an afternoon snack, where you can meet fellow guests, chat with your host or just relax in the pleasant luxury of the two sitting rooms.

INNKEEPERS:	Anne Stedman
ADDRESS:	802 North Main Avenue
	Newton, North Carolina 28658
TELEPHONE:	(828) 465-0404; (877) 435-7994
E-MAIL:	rents40@aol.com
WEBSITE:	www.trotthouse.com
ROOMS:	4 Rooms; 1 Suite; Private baths
CHILDREN:	Children age 12 and older welcome
ANIMALS:	Not allowed; Resident dog
HANDICAPPED:	Not handicapped accessible
DIETARY NEEDS:	Will accommodate guests' special dietary needs

Sausage in Puff Pastry

Makes 12 Servings

1	pound bulk pork sausage
1	medium onion, chopped
½	cup grated cheddar cheese
1	medium apple, peeled and grated
2	tablespoons chopped fresh sage or 2 teaspoons dried sage
1	(17-ounce) package frozen puff pastry, thawed
2	tablespoons milk

Preheat oven to 400°F. Brown sausage and onion in a skillet over medium heat, breaking up sausage as it cooks; drain well. Combine sausage mixture, cheese, apple and sage; mix well and set aside.

On a lightly floured surface, roll out 1 sheet of puff pastry into a 10x15-inch rectangle. Spread ½ of sausage mixture lengthwise down center of puff pastry. Cut puff pastry from edges to filling into 1-inch-wide strips. Fold alternating strips of puff pastry over filling in a criss-cross pattern. Brush ends with milk and seal. Repeat with remaining pastry and sausage mixture (if remaining pastry is too soft to handle, refrigerate for 5-10 minutes first).

Using 2 large spatulas, carefully transfer pastries to a greased baking pan or baking sheet. Brush pastries with remaining milk. Bake for 25-30 minutes, or until golden brown. Refrigerate leftovers.

Note: Unbaked pastry rolls can be wrapped and frozen for up to 1 week. Bake frozen pastry rolls for 30-38 minutes, or until golden brown.

The Lion & The Rose

The Lion & The Rose is located in the heart of the Montford Historic District. This beautiful pink lady, sitting at the top of a sloping lawn and gardens, offers privacy and enchantment amid luxurious surroundings. This is a place where you can indulge your romantic fantasies, enjoy decadent gourmet breakfasts and relish the comfort of luxury linens and feather beds. Your needs and wishes are not just met, they are anticipated.

Innkeeper Jim Palmer prides himself on his breakfasts, such as French toast stuffed with ricotta cheese, cream cheese and honey.

INNKEEPERS:	Jim and Linda Palmer
ADDRESS:	276 Montford Avenue
	Asheville, North Carolina 28801
TELEPHONE:	(828) 255-7673; (800) 546-6988
E-MAIL:	info@lion-rose.com
WEBSITE:	www.lion-rose.com
ROOMS:	4 Rooms; 1 Suite; Private baths
CHILDREN:	Children age 12 and older welcome
ANIMALS:	Not allowed; Resident dog
HANDICAPPED:	Not handicapped accessible
DIETARY NEEDS:	Will accommodate guests' special dietary needs

Corn Soufflé

1   (15-ounce) can corn, drained
1   (15-ounce) can creamed corn
1   (8½-ounce) box Jiffy corn muffin mix
1   large egg
2   tablespoons butter, melted
¼   teaspoon garlic powder
¼   teaspoon paprika

Preheat oven to 400°F. Combine all ingredients and pour into a greased 8x8-inch baking pan. Bake for 25 minutes, until lightly browned on top. Let stand for a few minutes, then slice and serve.

Barrister's

Enjoy Southern hospitality and a family atmosphere in one of Roxboro's most historic homes. Barrister's Bed & Breakfast is conveniently located near Raleigh-Durham and is two blocks from uptown Roxboro and the Person County History Museum.

This Georgian Revival home was built in 1921. Interesting architectural details include a grand staircase, handmade columns, beveled glass doors and mahogany beams in the foyer. Handpainted art is found on the dining room ceiling mural, family crest panels and living room cornice.

INNKEEPERS:	Cindy & Alan Hicks
ADDRESS:	400 North Main Street
	Roxboro, North Carolina 27573
TELEPHONE:	(336) 597-2848
E-MAIL:	barristersbedbreakfast@yahoo.com
WEBSITE:	www.barristersbedbreakfast.com
ROOMS:	3 Rooms; Private baths
CHILDREN:	Children age 10 and older welcome
ANIMALS:	Not allowed
HANDICAPPED:	Not handicapped accessible
DIETARY NEEDS:	Will accommodate guests' special dietary needs

Sunshine Orange Grits

Makes 4 Servings

"These are a hit with our Northern visitors." ~ Innkeeper, Barrister's Bed &
Breakfast

3	cups water
1	teaspoon salt
1	cup quick grits
1	cup no-pulp orange juice
½	stick butter
2	eggs
1	teaspoon grated orange zest
2	tablespoons packed brown sugar

Preheat oven to 350°F. Bring water and salt to a boil in a medium saucepan
over high heat. Stir in grits. Lower heat to medium and cook for 3 minutes,
stirring constantly. Remove from heat. Stir in orange juice, butter, eggs and
orange zest. Spoon grits mixture into a greased 1½-quart baking dish.
Sprinkle with brown sugar. Bake for 45 minutes, or until a knife inserted in
center comes out clean.

Appetizers, Side Dishes, Soups & Salads

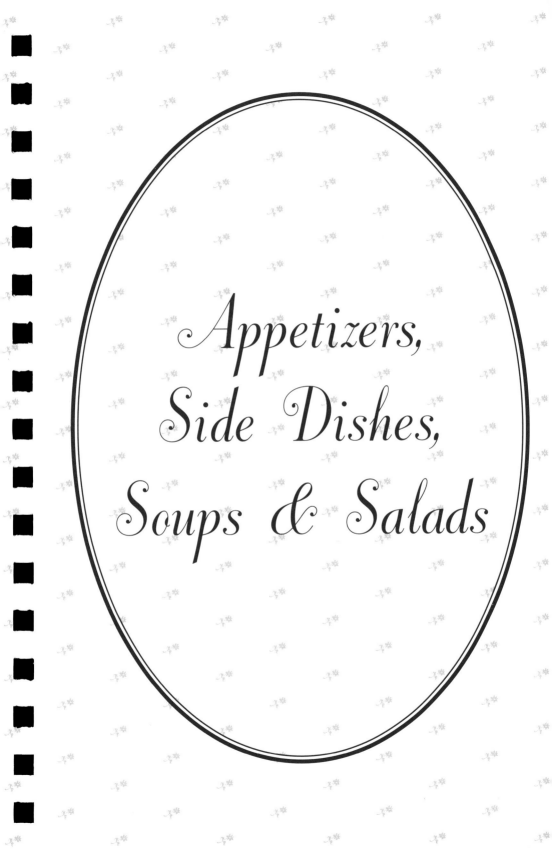

Appetizers,
Side Dishes,
Soups & Salads

Fuquay Mineral Spring Inn

The Fuquay Mineral Spring Inn & Garden is a Colonial Revival home listed as a local landmark in Wake County. The inn is located directly across the street from the historic Fuquay Mineral Spring Park and is convenient to Raleigh-Durham, Cary, Fayetteville and Chapel Hill, as well as such attractions as Exploris, Alltel Pavilion, Raven Rock State Park, the Carolina Hurricanes hockey team and more.

The inn is perched on a hill overlooking the spring and has a garden with a period gazebo offering great views of the town of Fuquay-Varina.

INNKEEPERS:	John & Patty Byrne
ADDRESS:	333 South Main Street
	Fuquay-Varina, North Carolina 27526
TELEPHONE:	(919) 552-3782; (866) 552-3782
E-MAIL:	jbyrne@fuquayinn.com
WEBSITE:	www.fuquayinn.com
ROOMS:	3 Rooms; 1 Suite; Private baths
CHILDREN:	Children age 12 and older welcome
ANIMALS:	Not allowed
HANDICAPPED:	Not handicapped accessible
DIETARY NEEDS:	Will accommodate guests' special dietary needs

Hot Jalapeño Crab Dip

Makes 4 to 6 Servings

1	pound lump crabmeat
1	teaspoon minced garlic
½	cup chopped pickled jalapeños (from a jar)
1	cup grated pepper Jack cheese
1	teaspoon Worcestershire sauce
1	tablespoon hot sauce
¼	teaspoon salt
½	cup mayonnaise
3	ounces Parmigiano-Reggiano cheese, grated

Crusty bread, for serving

Preheat oven to 350°F. In a medium bowl, combine crab, garlic, jalapeños, pepper Jack cheese, Worcestershire, hot sauce, salt and mayonnaise; toss gently to mix (take care not to break up lumps of crab). Spoon crab mixture into a shallow, medium baking dish. Sprinkle with Parmigiano-Reggiano cheese. Bake for about 25 minutes, until golden brown. Remove from oven and let stand for 5 minutes. Serve with crusty bread.

The Inn at Celebrity Dairy

Just a short drive from the cities in North Carolina's urban crescent, the Inn at Celebrity Dairy invites you to experience life lived at the pace of a small family farm. Sheltered on a gentle knoll under 250-year-old oak trees, the inn is actually comprised of two buildings – a modern Greek Revival farmhouse skirted by wide porches and the original settlers' 1800 log cabin.

Surrounding outbuildings attest to the farm's history – the original log hay barn and granary, 1880s smoke house, 1940s tobacco barns and, most recently, the farmstead goat dairy producing award-winning goat cheese.

INNKEEPERS:	Brit Pfann & John Bonitz
ADDRESS:	144 Celebrity Dairy Way
	Siler City, North Carolina 27344
TELEPHONE:	(919) 742-5176; (877) 742-5176
E-MAIL:	theinn@celebritydairy.com
WEBSITE:	www.celebritydairy.com
ROOMS:	7 Rooms; 1 Suite; Private & shared baths
CHILDREN:	Welcome
ANIMALS:	Not allowed; Resident outdoor cats & farm animals
HANDICAPPED:	Handicapped accessible
DIETARY NEEDS:	Will accommodate guests' special dietary needs

Black Bean, Goat Cheese & Tomatillo Three-Layer Dip

Makes 12 Servings

1   pound tomatillos, papery husks removed, washed, dried and quartered
2   cloves garlic, minced
3   medium jalapeño peppers, halved and seeded
1   teaspoon salt
Juice of ½ lemon
2   cups dehydrated black bean mix
2   cups boiling water
8   ounces goat cheese, crumbled
Cilantro leaves, for garnish
Tortilla chips, for serving

Put tomatillos, garlic, jalapeños, salt and lemon juice in a food processor; purée, then chill for at least 30 minutes (or overnight). Put black bean mix on a large platter (about 12-inches in diameter). Pour boiling water over black bean mix and stir with a fork until combined. Strain excess liquid from tomatillo mixture and spread over black beans. Top with crumbled goat cheese. Sprinkle with cilantro and serve with tortilla chips.

Arrowhead Inn

The Arrowhead Inn sits on six acres of gardens and lawns amid venerable magnolia and pecan trees. The inn, built in 1775 as a plantation home by the Lipscombe family, has been carefully renovated, while retaining the original moldings, wainscoting, mantelpieces and heart-of-pine wood floors. Each of the nine elegant guest rooms and the Carolina Log Cabin provide a serene respite with the amenities of a fine hotel.

A stone arrowhead marks the historic Great Indian Trading Path, traveled by Catawba and Waxhaw Indians between Virginia and the mountains.

INNKEEPERS:	Gloria & Phil Tebeo
ADDRESS:	106 Mason Road
	Durham, North Carolina 27712
TELEPHONE:	(800) 528-2207
E-MAIL:	info@arrowheadinn.com
WEBSITE:	www.arrowheadinn.com
ROOMS:	4 Rooms; 3 Suites; 2 Cottages; Private baths
CHILDREN:	Welcome
ANIMALS:	Not allowed
HANDICAPPED:	Handicapped accessible
DIETARY NEEDS:	Will accommodate guests' special dietary needs

Smoky Black Bean Dip

Makes 3 Cups

4 slices bacon
1 medium onion, chopped
1 red bell pepper, chopped
½ teaspoon ground cumin
½ teaspoon dried oregano
2 (15-ounce) cans black beans, drained
1 tablespoon chopped canned chipotle peppers
Salt and black pepper, to taste
½ cup sour cream
2 teaspoons chopped fresh cilantro
Tortilla chips, for serving

Cook bacon in a large skillet over medium heat until crisp; coarsely chop bacon and set aside. Pour off all but 1 tablespoon of bacon drippings from skillet. Add onion and bell pepper to skillet and cook for about 6 minutes, until onion is soft. Add cumin and oregano; cook for 1 minute. Add black beans and chipotle peppers. Lower heat to medium-low and simmer for about 4 minutes, stirring occasionally, until slightly thickened.

Transfer black bean mixture to a food processor or blender and process until smooth. Season with salt and pepper. Put black bean mixture in a bowl, cover and refrigerate for 2 hours. (The dip can be made up to 2 days ahead – cover and chill dip and bacon separately.)

Add ½ of bacon to dip and stir to combine. Top with sour cream. Sprinkle with cilantro and remaining bacon. Serve chilled or at room temperature with tortilla chips.

William Thomas House

The Gray Fish Richardson House, the historic name for the William Thomas House, was built in 1881 for Caro and Robert Gray. Robert Gray was an attorney, reporter and editor. In 1993, Jim and Sarah Lofton saw through the building's then commercial use and slightly down-at-the-heels appearance to envision a warm and welcoming bed & breakfast inn.

An extensive renovation has recaptured the warmth and spirit of Victorian days. The house reflects the quiet, genteel glow of Southern hospitality, as well as the practical comforts and conveniences of 21st century hostelries.

INNKEEPERS:	Jim & Sarah Lofton
ADDRESS:	530 North Blount Street
	Raleigh, North Carolina 27604
TELEPHONE:	(919) 755-9400; (800) 653-3466
E-MAIL:	lofton@williamthomashouse.com
WEBSITE:	www.williamthomashouse.com
ROOMS:	4 Rooms; Private baths
CHILDREN:	Welcome
ANIMALS:	Not allowed
HANDICAPPED:	Not handicapped accessible
DIETARY NEEDS:	Will accommodate guests' special dietary needs

Garlic Cheese Roll

Makes 8 to 10 Servings

1   (3-ounce) package cream cheese, softened
2   cups grated sharp cheddar cheese
1   clove garlic, minced
Dash of Tabasco sauce
Dash of cayenne pepper
Paprika
Crackers, for serving

Combine cream cheese, cheddar cheese, garlic, Tabasco and cayenne; shape into a ball. Roll in paprika until thoroughly covered. Serve with crackers.

The Verandas

Built in 1853, the mansion that houses the Verandas suffered extensive damage in a fire in 1992. Boarded up and decaying, the mansion was purchased by its present owners in 1995. After more than a year of complete renovation, the mansion was then professionally decorated with English and American antiques as well as traditional furniture.

The AAA Four Diamond Verandas offers eight large guestrooms – all are corner rooms. Bathrooms have garden-size soaking tubs with shower, marble floors and vanity tops and custom wainscoting and vanities.

INNKEEPERS:	Dennis Madsen & Charles Pennington
ADDRESS:	202 Nun Street
	Wilmington, North Carolina 28401
TELEPHONE:	(910) 251-2212
E-MAIL:	verandas4@aol.com
WEBSITE:	www.verandas.com
ROOMS:	8 Rooms; Private baths
CHILDREN:	Children age 12 and older welcome
ANIMALS:	Not allowed; Resident cat
HANDICAPPED:	Not handicapped accessible
DIETARY NEEDS:	Will accommodate guests' special dietary needs

The Verandas Caviar Pie

Makes 1 Pie

"This appetizer is easy to make, elegant and oh-so good! Plan ahead, it needs to be refrigerated for at least 4 hours or overnight." ~ Innkeeper, The Verandas

1½   cups sour cream
1   (8-ounce) package cream cheese, softened
1   medium or large sweet onion, finely minced
8   hard-boiled eggs, peeled and coarsely chopped
¼   cup mayonnaise
1   teaspoon dry mustard
1   teaspoon celery seeds
Black or white pepper, to taste
Dash of Worcestershire sauce
Dash of Tabasco sauce
1   (3-ounce) container caviar
Lemon pinwheels, for serving
Fresh toast points, for serving

Blend sour cream and cream cheese in a blender until smooth. Line a 9-inch round cake pan with plastic wrap. With a spatula, evenly spread sour cream mixture about ½-inch-thick over plastic wrap (consistency should be a little on the thick side). Spread onions over sour cream mixture.

Combine eggs, mayonnaise, mustard, celery seed, pepper, Worcestershire and Tabasco, making the best egg salad sandwich mixture you can – the mixture should be on the drier side (don't add salt). Spread egg mixture over onions (pan should be filled to the brim). Put plastic wrap over layers in pan and pat smooth. Refrigerate for at least 4 hours or overnight.

To serve, remove plastic wrap from pan and place a beautiful dish (not silver, as it will tarnish) upside-down on top of pan. Invert pan and remove bottom layer of plastic wrap. Drain caviar in a colander until fairly dry. With the back of a spoon, spread caviar evenly over top of pie. Garnish with lemon pinwheels. Serve with toast points.

Lamplight Inn

The Lamplight Inn shares a 150-year-old tobacco farm with the Tobacco Farm Camp. The secluded camp area is surrounded by woods and tobacco fields. It is set away from the road and the noise, but is an easy drive to stores and highways. Nestled in the woods with lots of open space, you can bring your children and your pets. Relax in a hammock or porch swing on the barn porch or the corn crib-screened gazebo.

The camp offers electric hookups for boats and trollers, a nearby boat ramp and picnic tables and fire pits under spreading old oak trees.

INNKEEPERS:	Shirley Payne
ADDRESS:	1680 Flemingtown Road
	Henderson, North Carolina 27537
TELEPHONE:	(252) 438-6311; (877) 222-0100
E-MAIL:	inn@lamplightbandb.com
WEBSITE:	www.lamplightbandb.com
ROOMS:	4 Rooms; Private baths
CHILDREN:	Welcome
ANIMALS:	Call ahead
HANDICAPPED:	Handicapped accessible
DIETARY NEEDS:	Will accommodate guests' special dietary needs

Festive Oyster Casserole

Makes 12 Servings

"This has been my Christmas Eve dish for years. I love sharing it with friends because it is so special." ~ Innkeeper, Lamplight Inn

1	quart oysters, drained
16	soda crackers, crushed
1	(10-ounce) package frozen chopped spinach, thawed and drained
1	cup chopped celery
½	cup chopped onion
1	(4-ounce) jar pimentos, chopped
¼	cup lemon juice
½	teaspoon paprika
1	tablespoon Worcestershire sauce
1	teaspoon salt

Buttered cracker crumbs, for topping

Preheat oven to 350°F. Toss together all ingredients, except buttered cracker crumbs, in a casserole dish or a 9x13-inch baking dish. Top with buttered cracker crumbs. Bake for 30 minutes.

Little Warren

The circa 1913 Inn at Little Warren features spacious rooms, 13-foot ceilings and an inviting wrap-around porch. With a welcoming fire in winter and a spacious porch for summer, every courtesy is extended to guests.

Innkeeper Tom Miller is the inn's chef. His breakfasts range from expanded continental to elegant Southern or English repasts. All are beautifully presented on silver, china, crystal and fine table linens. Innkeeper Patsy Miller feels right at home as an innkeeper as she was raised in her family's small Virginia Beach hotel.

INNKEEPERS:	Patsy & Tom Miller
ADDRESS:	304 East Park Avenue
	Tarboro, North Carolina 27886
TELEPHONE:	(252) 823-1314; (800) 309-1314
E-MAIL:	lwarrenbb@tarboronc.com
WEBSITE:	www.bbonline.com/nc/littlewarren
ROOMS:	3 Rooms; Private baths
CHILDREN:	Children age 6 and older welcome
ANIMALS:	Not allowed
HANDICAPPED:	Not handicapped accessible
DIETARY NEEDS:	Will accommodate guests' special dietary needs

Creole String Beans

Makes 4 to 6 Servings

"In 1960, a California neighbor shared this with me, a bride with Carolina roots." ~ Innkeeper, Little Warren Bed & Breakfast

4	slices bacon, chopped
1	onion, sliced
1	(15-ounce) can stewed tomatoes
1	tablespoon all-purpose flour
¾	cup water

Tabasco sauce, to taste

2	(10-ounce) boxes frozen French string beans, thawed and drained

Preheat oven to 350°F. Cook bacon in a skillet over medium heat. Remove bacon and set aside; reserve bacon drippings in skillet. Add onion to skillet and cook until soft. Combine tomatoes, flour and water; stir into onions in skillet. Stir in Tabasco and string beans. Put string bean mixture in a greased 1½-quart casserole dish and sprinkle with bacon. Bake for 30 minutes.

Albemarle Inn

The only Asheville bed & breakfast awarded the AAA Four Diamond rating, the Albemarle Inn is listed on the National Register of Historic Places and was described as "the cream of the crop" by Lodging.com.

The innkeepers have recreated a life of gracious comfort rarely found today. Sip morning coffee, tea or chocolate in the privacy of the Sunrise Suite's enclosed porch. Take an evening stroll through the beautifully landscaped gardens. After visiting the area's superb attractions, return to the inn and relax in the quiet elegance of the downstairs parlor.

INNKEEPERS:	Cathy & Larry Sklar
ADDRESS:	86 Edgemont Road
	Asheville, North Carolina 28801
TELEPHONE:	(828) 255-0027; (800) 621-7435
E-MAIL:	info@albemarleinn.com
WEBSITE:	www.albemarleinn.com
ROOMS:	9 Rooms; 2 Suites; Private baths
CHILDREN:	Children age 12 and older welcome
ANIMALS:	Not allowed; Resident dogs
HANDICAPPED:	Not handicapped accessible
DIETARY NEEDS:	Will accommodate guests' special dietary needs

Roasted Red Pepper Sauce

Makes About 1½ Cups

Serve with Ruffled Crêpes (see recipe on page 97)

1   (16-ounce) jar roasted sweet red peppers
1   teaspoon onion powder
1   tablespoon extra-virgin olive oil
1   teaspoon lemon juice, or to taste
2   tablespoons vegetable or chicken broth or water (or more for
     a thinner sauce)
½   teaspoon cumin
Salt and black pepper, to taste

In a blender or food processor, combine all ingredients and blend until smooth and creamy.

Note: This sauce will keep covered and refrigerated for up to 4 days.

The Inn at Celebrity Dairy

G loria – the Celebrity Dairy's "spokesgoat" – welcomes you to the inn. Here, you'll meet her chorus line of 100 "hoofers" at the Goat Hilton when they assemble for twice daily milking. Following time-honored French farmstead techniques, the milk is transformed into fresh chèvre

Its taste is inextricably tied to its place of origin – the dairy's particular herd of Alpine and Saanen goats, their forage unique to the farm's pasture and woods, the Piedmont's gentle seasons and an evolving skill in transforming the continuously changing milk into a delicate fresh chèvre.

INNKEEPERS:	Brit Pfann & John Bonitz
ADDRESS:	144 Celebrity Dairy Way
	Siler City, North Carolina 27344
TELEPHONE:	(919) 742-5176; (877) 742-5176
E-MAIL:	theinn@celebritydairy.com
WEBSITE:	www.celebritydairy.com
ROOMS:	7 Rooms; 1 Suite; Private & shared baths
CHILDREN:	Welcome
ANIMALS:	Not allowed; Resident outdoor cats & farm animals
HANDICAPPED:	Handicapped accessible
DIETARY NEEDS:	Will accommodate guests' special dietary needs

Butternut Squash Soup

Makes 10 Servings

"We serve this soup topped with fresh goat yogurt or goat curd thinned to the consistency of heavy cream." ~ Innkeeper, Inn at Celebrity Dairy

1	large butternut squash
2	tablespoons vegetable oil
2	medium onions, chopped
2	cloves garlic, minced
1	large red bell pepper, minced
½	teaspoon cumin
½	teaspoon coriander
½	teaspoon ground ginger
½	teaspoon dry mustard
½	teaspoon curry powder
1½	teaspoons salt
1	cup orange juice

Juice and grated zest of 1 lemon

¼	teaspoon cayenne pepper or hot sauce
1	(14½-ounce) can corn, drained

Fresh goat yogurt or curd (thinned to consistency of heavy cream), for serving

Preheat oven to 425°F. Cut squash in half lengthwise and scoop out seeds. Put squash in a baking dish with 1-inch of water. Bake for about 1 hour, until tender. Peel and cube squash, then purée in a food processor or blender in batches (using 1 cup of squash and up to 1 cup of squash cooking liquid or water to thin per batch).

Heat oil in a skillet over medium heat. Add onions, garlic and bell pepper; cook until onions are translucent. Transfer squash and onion mixture to a soup pot. Add cumin, coriander, ginger, mustard, curry powder and salt. Bring to a boil, lower heat and simmer for 20 minutes. Add orange and lemon juices, lemon zest, cayenne and corn. Simmer for 10 minutes. Serve topped with goat yogurt or curd (be careful, this soup retains a lot of heat, so don't serve it too hot).

Folkestone Inn

What better way to cap off a day in the beautiful mountains than with a gourmet dinner – and never leave your lodgings. The Folkestone Inn has long been known for its scrumptious breakfasts, and the innkeepers are now offering guests a fine dining experience on Saturday nights.

Menus are seasonal. A summer dinner might include chilled avocado soup, tomato, basil and mozzarella salad with balsamic vinegar, fresh mountain trout or chicken à la Folkestone, sautéed summer squash, sorbet intermezzo, peach shortcake and chocolates.

INNKEEPERS:	Peggy Myles & Kay Creighton
ADDRESS:	101 Folkestone Road
	Bryson City, North Carolina 28713
TELEPHONE:	(828) 488-2730; (888) 812-3385
E-MAIL:	innkeeper@folkestone.com
WEBSITE:	www.folkestone.com
ROOMS:	10 Rooms; Private baths
CHILDREN:	Children age 10 and older welcome
ANIMALS:	Dogs and horses welcome; Resident cats
HANDICAPPED:	Not handicapped accessible
DIETARY NEEDS:	Will accommodate guests' special dietary needs

Chilled Avocado Soup

Makes 6 Servings

"This easy soup has been a summer favorite with our Saturday night dinner guests. It has quickly become our most requested recipe. Even people who don't particularly like avocados love this soup." ~ Innkeeper, Folkestone Inn

3   large ripe avocados
1   small onion, chopped
Juice of 1 lemon, divided
1   (14½-ounce) can low-sodium, low-fat chicken broth
1   cup heavy cream
Salt and black pepper, to taste
Thinly sliced avocado, cilantro sprigs and/or crème fraîche, for garnish

Cut avocados in half, remove pits and scoop flesh into a food processor. Add onion and ½ of lemon juice; pulse to purée, then transfer mixture to a large bowl. Stir in chicken broth. Stir in cream. Season with remaining lemon juice, salt and pepper. Cover and chill.

To serve, ladle soup into small bowls. Garnish by either floating thin slices of avocado or a cilantro leaf in soup. For a really festive presentation, add a dollop of crème fraîche to center of soup and gently put a cilantro leaf in center of crème fraîche. Prepare yourself for the oohs and aahs!

Lamplight Inn

Located 45 minutes from the Raleigh-Durham airport, the Lamplight Inn sits on a 150-year-old, five-acre tobacco farm. Let the innkeeper beckon you with the soft glow of the many chimney lamps used to light this restored farm. Relax on the wrap-around porch or stroll the grounds.

A short drive will bring you to the Kerr Lake State Recreation Area to enjoy sailing, fishing, water skiing and hiking on a 50,000-acre, man-made lake. More than 800 miles of wooded shoreline provide access to a variety of fun-filled activities.

INNKEEPERS:	Shirley Payne
ADDRESS:	1680 Flemingtown Road
	Henderson, North Carolina 27537
TELEPHONE:	(252) 438-6311; (877) 222-0100
E-MAIL:	inn@lamplightbandb.com
WEBSITE:	www.lamplightbandb.com
ROOMS:	4 Rooms; Private baths
CHILDREN:	Welcome
ANIMALS:	Call ahead
HANDICAPPED:	Handicapped accessible
DIETARY NEEDS:	Will accommodate guests' special dietary needs

Chicken & Wild Rice Salad

Makes 6 to 8 Servings

"A lovely blend of favors. Canned tuna may be substituted for the chicken. Plan ahead, this salad needs to marinate overnight." ~ Innkeeper, Lamplight Inn

1   package Good Seasons Italian dressing mix
2   (10-ounce) packages Uncle Ben's wild rice mix
1   cup mayonnaise
5   boneless, skinless chicken breasts, cooked and cut up
1   (4-ounce) jar pimentos
1   (6-ounce) jar water-packed artichoke hearts, drained
2   cups finely chopped celery
2   cups finely chopped green bell pepper
1   (10½-ounce) package frozen peas (optional)
1   pound fresh mushrooms, sliced

Prepare salad dressing and cook rice according to package directions. Mix salad dressing, rice, mayonnaise and chicken; cover and refrigerate overnight.

The next day, stir pimentos, artichokes, celery, bell pepper and peas into rice mixture. Stir in mushrooms not more than 30 minutes before serving.

Luncheon & Dinner Entrées

Luncheon & Dinner Entrées

Folkestone Inn

Welcome to the Folkestone Inn and all the quiet comforts of this 1920s mountain farmhouse. A sunny porch. A walk in the woods. A good book. A warm bath. A cozy bed. A hearty breakfast. A place to build friendships. A place to refresh the spirit.

The Folkestone Inn was founded in 1977. It retains all the warmth and charm of the old family homestead, from the pot-bellied stove in the parlor, to the period decor, to the cozy guest rooms with antique beds, to the morning aromas of bacon, muffins and coffee drifting through the house.

INNKEEPERS:	Peggy Myles & Kay Creighton
ADDRESS:	101 Folkestone Road
	Bryson City, North Carolina 28713
TELEPHONE:	(828) 488-2730; (888) 812-3385
E-MAIL:	innkeeper@folkestone.com
WEBSITE:	www.folkestone.com
ROOMS:	10 Rooms; Private baths
CHILDREN:	Children age 10 and older welcome
ANIMALS:	Dogs and horses welcome; Resident cats
HANDICAPPED:	Not handicapped accessible
DIETARY NEEDS:	Will accommodate guests' special dietary needs

Roasted Chicken with Fried Apples & Caramelized Onions

Makes 4 Servings

"We serve this chicken with mashed sweet potatoes and green beans." ~ Innkeeper, Folkestone Inn

3	large yellow onions, divided
4	pounds Granny Smith apples, divided
1	stick butter, divided
1	roasting chicken (large enough for 4 servings)
1	tablespoon sugar
2	tablespoons Calvados or other apple brandy (optional)
1	teaspoon salt

Preheat oven to 400°F. Quarter 1 onion and 1 apple and stuff into chicken. Melt 4 tablespoons of butter; brush chicken with some of the butter. Roast chicken, basting with melted butter every 30 minutes, for about 90 minutes, or until juices run clear and chicken is done.

Melt 2 tablespoons of butter in a skillet over medium-low heat. Slice remaining 2 onions, add to butter and cook for about 10 minutes, until onions are a rich, golden brown; set aside.

Peel, core and slice remaining apples. Melt 2 tablespoons of butter in a skillet over low heat. Add apples and sugar. Cook, stirring occasionally, until apples are soft but still hold their shape. Stir in Calvados. Stir in onions and salt; cook for 2-3 minutes to blend flavors.

Divide apple mixture among 4 plates. Cut chicken into quarters and place on top of apple mixture on each plate.

Maxwell House

Welcome to the Maxwell House Bed & Breakfast at the Historic Merritt House, a beautiful brick and granite Victorian home built in 1901. Southern hospitality abounds. The inn is 30 miles from Winston-Salem, 20 minutes from Pilot Mountain State Park and 15 miles from the Blue Ridge Parkway.

The house consists of 12 large rooms with 10- and 11-foot ceilings and beautiful oak and pine woodwork. All of the rooms are decorated with antiques from local shops and family pieces and memorabilia.

INNKEEPERS:	Twyla & Roger Sickmiller
ADDRESS:	618 North Main Street
	Mt. Airy, North Carolina 27030
TELEPHONE:	(336) 786-2174; (877) 786-2174
E-MAIL:	maxwellhousebb@hotmail.com
WEBSITE:	www.bbonline.com/nc/maxwellhouse
ROOMS:	4 Rooms; Private baths
CHILDREN:	Children age 12 and older welcome
ANIMALS:	Not allowed
HANDICAPPED:	Handicapped accessible; 1 room
DIETARY NEEDS:	Will accommodate guests' special dietary needs

Hawaiian Chicken with Pineapple Rum Sauce

Makes 5 to 6 Servings

"Think you are too busy to have a great meal? This is one of those festive dishes that can be made the night before and just "plugged" in before you leave for work or just play for the day." ~ Innkeeper, Maxwell House Bed & Breakfast

2	cups uncooked long grain rice
3	pounds cut-up chicken (thighs work well)
1	cup chopped onions or leeks
2	cloves garlic, minced
1	teaspoon salt
1	teaspoon dried oregano or 1 tablespoon chopped fresh oregano
½	cup raisins
1	(20-ounce) can crushed pineapple with juice
½	cup rum
4	cups water

Lightly grease sides and bottom of a large crock pot with shortening.* Add rice to crock pot. Top with chicken. Top with onions and garlic.

In a large bowl, combine salt, oregano, raisins, pineapple with juice, rum and water (if making this the night before, reserve this mixture until you are ready to cook); pour over ingredients in crock pot. Turn crock pot to low and cook for 8-9 hours.

Have a laughingly great day. When you arrive home, dinner is fork tender and ready. Add a salad with Mandarin oranges and coconut or some veggies and you are ready to serve.

*Note: This dish can be made in a large roasting pan covered tightly with a lid or foil and baked in a preheated 225°F for 8-9 hours.

Inn on Main Street

Western North Carolina is a mecca for outdoors enthusiasts. There are thousands of miles of trophy trout streams joining rivers where whitewater rafters and kayakers can take in the mountain beauty up close. Where highland valleys meet climbing hills, some of the most beautiful golf courses in the nation challenge all skill levels and inn guests get a discount at Reems Creek Golf Club, which is one of the best.

An hour west of the inn, Great Smoky Mountains National Park contains more plant and animal species than any other national park in America.

INNKEEPERS:	Dan & Nancy Ward
ADDRESS:	88 South Main Street
	Weaverville, North Carolina 28787
TELEPHONE:	(828) 645-4935; (877) 873-6074
E-MAIL:	relax@innonmain.com
WEBSITE:	www.innonmain.com
ROOMS:	7 Rooms; Private baths
CHILDREN:	Children age 12 and older welcome
ANIMALS:	Not allowed; Resident outdoor dog
HANDICAPPED:	Not handicapped accessible
DIETARY NEEDS:	Will accommodate guests' special dietary needs

Pollo Pibil

Makes 6 Servings

"This traditional Yucatecan dish goes well with black beans and rice, Mexican lime soup and sweet potatoes. This is not a spicy dish. You can serve it with salsa, but it is not traditional." ~ Innkeeper, Inn on Main Street

6   boneless chicken breast halves
4   teaspoons achiote powder (or ½ (3-ounce) jar adobo paste)*
1   medium onion, chopped
1   bell pepper, chopped
½   cup sour orange juice or orange juice
3   large banana leaves, cut in half*

Preheat oven to 350°F. Coat chicken with achiote powder. Put chicken in a non-reactive (glass or plastic) bowl. Add onion, bell pepper and sour orange juice; turn chicken to coat, cover and refrigerate for 1 hour or more. Wrap each chicken breast in ½ banana leaf. Put chicken in a baking pan and top with orange juice mixture and onion and bell pepper. Bake for about 30 minutes, until done, or wrap in foil and smoke or grill.

*Note: Achiote powder, adobo paste and banana leaves are available in the Mexican food section of some larger groceries and Mexican and specialty markets.

Knollwood House

Your visit to the Sandhills of North Carolina is not complete without a stay at the elegant Knollwood House. This gracious and stately home, built in 1927 as a holiday retreat for a wealthy Philadelphia family, has been totally renovated and artfully restored by its present owners, Dick and Mimi Beatty, who opened Knollwood House in 1991.

Set on five acres, amidst azaleas, holly trees, long-leaf pines and towering magnolias, this English manor-style home is as beautifully decorated within as it is landscaped without.

INNKEEPERS:	Mimi & Dick Beatty
ADDRESS:	1495 West Connecticut Avenue
	Southern Pines, North Carolina 28387
TELEPHONE:	(910) 692-9390
E-MAIL:	knollwood@pinehurst.net
WEBSITE:	www.knollwoodhouse.com
ROOMS:	2 Rooms; 4 Suites; Private baths
CHILDREN:	Welcome
ANIMALS:	Not allowed; Resident cat
HANDICAPPED:	Handicapped accessible
DIETARY NEEDS:	Will accommodate guests' special dietary needs

Chicken Hash

Makes 6 Servings

"A Sunday brunch favorite. Returning guests tell me they eagerly look forward to this dish. The recipe is easily doubled, tripled, etc., and it freezes well, too." - Innkeeper, Knollwood House

1   (6-ounce) package Uncle Ben's long grain and wild rice mix
1   tablespoon plus ½ stick butter
8   ounces mushrooms, sliced
½   cup chopped onion
⅓   cup all-purpose flour
1   teaspoon salt
Black pepper, to taste
1   cup chicken broth
1   cup sour cream
2   cups chopped cooked chicken
5   strips bacon, cooked and crumbled (optional)

Preheat oven to 350°F. Cook rice according to package directions. Melt 1 tablespoon of butter in a skillet over medium heat. Add mushrooms and cook until softened; set aside.

Melt the ½ stick of butter in a skillet over medium heat. Add onions and cook until soft. Stir in flour, salt and pepper. Slowly add broth, stirring constantly. Slowly add sour cream, stirring constantly. Add chicken, rice and mushrooms; stir to combine.

Put chicken mixture in a lightly greased 2-quart casserole and bake for 60 minutes. Scatter bacon on top of hash after 45 minutes of baking time.

Note: This dish freezes well unbaked, just bring it to room temperature before baking.

1900 Inn on Montford

Upon entering the inn you will be met by resident cat, Allie, the official greeter. The foyer, with its stone fireplace, leads to a formal living room, library and sunroom, filled with seasonal plants and palms. A porch, which spans the front of the inn, is adorned with wicker furniture.

The inn is filled with Georgian and Victorian antiques and Persian carpets. It is a gracious backdrop for the owners' collection of Victorian silver napkin rings, tea caddies, Staffordshire pottery, English county maps, Baxter prints and period cut glass, which represent 30 years of avid collecting.

INNKEEPERS:	Ron & Lynn Carlson
ADDRESS:	296 Montford
	Asheville, North Carolina 28801
TELEPHONE:	(828) 254-9569; (800) 254-9569
E-MAIL:	info@innonmontford.com
WEBSITE:	www.innonmontford.com
ROOMS:	4 Rooms; 1 Suite; Private baths
CHILDREN:	Children age 12 and older welcome
ANIMALS:	Not allowed; Resident cat
HANDICAPPED:	Not handicapped accessible
DIETARY NEEDS:	Will accommodate guests' special dietary needs

Volaille Au Gratin

Makes 4 Servings

"'Volaille' is a French word referring to chicken used to prepare a dish. Thus, 'volaille au gratin' is chicken au gratin." ~ Innkeeper, 1900 Inn on Montford

4	tablespoons butter, divided
1½	cups coarsely grated onion
2¼	cups chicken broth
1	cup rice, uncooked
½	teaspoon dried thyme
3	large bay leaves
1	tablespoon chopped fresh parsley
2¼	cups cubed cooked chicken
2	tablespoons all-purpose flour
1	cup light cream or half & half
1	teaspoon salt
½	teaspoon white pepper
¾	cup grated Gruyère or Swiss cheese

Paprika, for garnish

Preheat oven to 400°F. Melt 2 tablespoons of butter in a saucepan over medium heat. Add onions and cook until soft. Add broth, rice, thyme, bay leaves and parsley. Cover and bring to boil. Lower heat and simmer for 20 minutes (do not uncover pan as it will keep rice from cooking properly). Put rice mixture in a buttered casserole dish and remove bay leaves. Top with chicken.

Melt remaining 2 tablespoons of butter in a saucepan over medium heat. Add flour and cook, stirring, for 90 seconds. Gradually whisk in cream and bring to a simmer, stirring constantly. Remove from heat. Add salt, pepper and cheese. Return to heat and cook, stirring, for 5 minutes. Pour cream mixture over ingredients in casserole. Sprinkle with paprika and bake for 10-15 minutes.

Lodges on Lake Lure

A long the shores of majestic Lake Lure, you can golf, hike, boat, fish, ride horses or just lounge and be spoiled at the Lodges at Lake Lure. An elegant getaway, the lodge is furnished with art, antiques and collectibles and offers fabulous views, stone fireplaces, terraces and distinctive dining.

The lodge is a wonderful combination of an elegant country inn and a casual bed & breakfast – an intimate environment with all the privacy you want. It is a large, rambling structure, situated high on the hillside to afford a sweeping view of the lake and beyond.

INNKEEPERS:	Gisela Hopke
ADDRESS:	361 Charlotte Drive
	Lake Lure, North Carolina 28746
TELEPHONE:	(828) 625-2789; (800) 733-2785
E-MAIL:	info@lodgeonlakelure.com
WEBSITE:	www.lodgeonlakelure.com
ROOMS:	17 Rooms; Private baths
CHILDREN:	Children age 8 and older welcome
ANIMALS:	Not allowed; Resident cat
HANDICAPPED:	Handicapped accessible
DIETARY NEEDS:	Will accommodate guests' special dietary needs

Mark's Marinated Quail with Basil-Infused Honey

Makes 4 to 8 Servings

4-8 European boned quail (partially boned)
½ medium yellow onion, sliced into half rounds
2 cloves garlic
1-2 sprigs fresh rosemary
1 bay leaf
4-6 black peppercorns
¼ cup balsamic vinegar
Extra-virgin olive oil
Salt and black pepper, to taste
¼ cup clover honey
¼ cup hot water
8-10 fresh basil leaves
¾ teaspoon crushed red pepper flakes

Put quail in a small baking dish. Combine onion, garlic, rosemary, bay leaf, peppercorns, balsamic vinegar and enough olive oil to cover quail; pour over quail, cover and refrigerate for at least 4 hours and up to 24 hours.

Preheat oven to 350°F. Remove quail from marinade; shake off excess marinade. Season with salt and pepper, then sear both sides of quail in a skillet (or on a grill) over high heat. Transfer quail to oven and roast for 10-12 minutes, or until cooked through.

While quail are roasting, combine honey, water, basil and red pepper flakes in a small saucepan over medium-low heat. Cook for 10-12 minutes (be careful not to burn honey), then strain. When quail are done, let rest for several minutes, then glaze with honey mixture. Serve 2 quail per person with mushroom risotto and asparagus as an entrée or 1 quail per person with blue cheese-stuffed roasted red bliss potatoes as an appetizer

Herren House

You can't have a great bed & breakfast inn without a great breakfast. At the Herren House, breakfast is exceptional, complete with music, hand-ironed linens, fine china, casual conversation and candlelight.

A special part of breakfast is one of a dozen varieties of homemade chicken sausage, such as dried cherry and toasted almond or sun-dried tomato and pine nut. Entrées may include eggs with herbs from the inn's garden or oatmeal pancakes with North Carolina peach sauce. French apple butter muffins, almond coffee cake and chocolate cinnamon rolls are heavenly.

INNKEEPERS:	Jerry & Tom Halsey
ADDRESS:	94 East Street
	Waynesville, North Carolina 28786
TELEPHONE:	(828) 452-7837; (800) 284-1932
E-MAIL:	herren@brinet.com
WEBSITE:	www.herrenhouse.com
ROOMS:	6 Rooms; Private baths
CHILDREN:	Children age 12 and older welcome
ANIMALS:	Not allowed; Resident dog
HANDICAPPED:	Handicapped accessible
DIETARY NEEDS:	Will accommodate guests' special dietary needs

Blackberry-Glazed Pork Tenderloin

Makes 8 Servings

2	(1-pound) pork tenderloins
⅓	cup olive oil
2	tablespoons chopped fresh rosemary
1½	teaspoons dried sage
1	teaspoon salt
½	teaspoon black pepper
¾	cup seedless blackberry jam
¼	cup sweet vermouth

Put pork in a heavy-duty zipper plastic bag. Whisk together oil, rosemary, sage, salt and pepper; add to pork, seal bag and shake gently to coat pork. Refrigerate for at least 4 hours.

Preheat oven to 450°F. Remove pork from bag and place in a roasting pan. Roast for 15 minutes. Meanwhile, combine jam and vermouth in a small saucepan over low heat. Cook, stirring frequently, until jam is melted and mixture is smooth. Transfer ½ of jam mixture to a bowl.

After pork has roasted for 15 minutes, lower oven temperature to 300°F and continue roasting pork, basting every 10-15 minutes with jam mixture in saucepan, until a meat thermometer reads 150°F (about 20-30 minutes longer). Remove pork from oven, tent with foil and let rest for 15 minutes. Warm jam in bowl and serve on the side with the pork.

Earthshine Mountain Lodge

Resting atop one of the grandest ridges in the Appalachians, Earthshine Mountain Lodge is the storybook country inn of your imagination. Open year-round for families or groups, the lodge is located between Brevard and Cashiers in the famed Toxaway resort area.

"We visited Earthshine last summer. Since then, we have vacationed at Yosemite, Universal Studios/Disney World, Vail and Gatlinburg, and when asking my son where he wanted to vacation next, he replied without hesitation, 'Back to Earthshine!'" ~ Susan Guidry, *Family Vacationer*

INNKEEPERS:	Kim Heinitsh & Marion Boatwright
ADDRESS:	Route 1, Box 216-C
	Lake Toxaway, North Carolina 28747
TELEPHONE:	(828) 862-4207
E-MAIL:	earthshine@citcom.net
WEBSITE:	www.earthshinemtnlodge.com
ROOMS:	10 Rooms; 3 Suites; Private baths
CHILDREN:	Welcome
ANIMALS:	Not allowed; Resident sheep, goats & horses
HANDICAPPED:	Handicapped accessible
DIETARY NEEDS:	Will accommodate guests' special dietary needs

Stuffed Pork Chops

Makes 7 Servings

"There is nothing like these chops!" ~ Innkeeper, Earthshine Mountain Lodge

1   tablespoon butter or olive oil
½   onion, chopped
1   tablespoon chopped fresh sage
1   stalk celery, chopped
½   apple, peeled and chopped
Pinch of salt
Pinch of black pepper
Pinch of parsley
½   baked (8x8-inch) cornbread, crumbled (or other bread)
1   egg
14   (1-inch-thick) pork chops

Melt butter in a small skillet over medium heat. Add onion, sage, celery and apple; cook until soft. Transfer onion mixture to a bowl and stir in salt, pepper, parsley, crumbled cornbread and egg; mix well. Adjust seasonings, if needed.

Preheat oven to 450°F. Create a pocket in each pork chop by slicing chops down the center; stuff with cornbread mixture. Bake in a baking pan for 45-60 minutes, or until done.

The Duke Mansion

From the moment you enter the Grand Hall, walk across the original marble floors and see the beautiful gardens through the French doors, you know that you have entered a special place.

Guest rooms at the Duke Mansion are a wonderful blend of Southern charm and elegance with modern comfort and conveniences. Enjoy a room with a traditional sleeping porch or awake in a cozy tree-top room. Exquisite linens, luxurious robes and fine toiletries pamper you, and you are bid good night with a gourmet bedside treat.

INNKEEPERS:	The Lynnwood Foundation
ADDRESS:	400 Hermitage Road
	Charlotte, North Carolina 28207
TELEPHONE:	(704) 714-4400; (888) 202-1009
E-MAIL:	frontdesk@tlwf.com
WEBSITE:	www.dukemansion.org
ROOMS:	20 Rooms; Private baths
CHILDREN:	Welcome
ANIMALS:	Not allowed; Resident cats
HANDICAPPED:	Handicapped accessible
DIETARY NEEDS:	Will accommodate guests' special dietary needs

Pan-Fried North Carolina Brook Trout with Beurre Blanc

Makes 4 Servings

For the beurre blanc:
1   teaspoon olive oil
1   teaspoon minced shallots
1   cup white wine
1   teaspoon fresh lime juice
¾   cup diced, peeled, seeded small green zebra tomatoes
1   stick butter, cut into pieces (as needed)

For the trout:
1   cup all-purpose flour
1   teaspoon chopped parsley
Kosher salt and black pepper, to taste
Dash of cayenne pepper
Dash of granulated garlic
2   butterflied brook or rainbow trout, split
½   stick butter
Sweet potato, artichoke & crawfish hash, for serving (see page 155)

For the beurre blanc: Heat oil in a small skillet over medium heat. Add shallots and cook until soft. Add wine and lime juice. Bring to a boil, lower heat and simmer until reduced by half. Add tomatoes and enough butter to form a sauce thick enough to coat a spoon. Keep warm.

For the trout: Preheat oven to 350°F. Combine flour, parsley, salt, pepper, cayenne and granulated garlic. Dredge trout in flour mixture. Melt butter in a large, oven-proof skillet over medium heat. Add trout to skillet, flesh-side-down, and cook until lightly browned. Turn trout, transfer skillet to oven and bake for 4 minutes.

To serve: Fill a ⅓ cup measure with sweet potato hash and invert over center of a plate. Cut a trout fillet in half crossways and arrange on top of hash. Drizzle beurre blanc around outside of plate and serve.

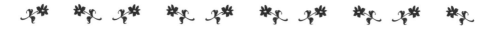

Fuquay Mineral Spring Inn

Innkeepers John (the mayor of Fuquay-Varina) and Patty (an English teacher at Fuquay-Varina High School) welcome you to the Fuquay Mineral Spring Inn & Garden after two years of detailed restoration.

Fuquay Mineral Spring was discovered in 1858 by Davey Crocket Fuquay and Stephen Fuquay while plowing on their father's farm. The spring was believed to have healing powers and visitors came from far and wide to partake of the mineral waters and to vacation and relax.

INNKEEPERS:	John & Patty Byrne
ADDRESS:	333 South Main Street
	Fuquay-Varina, North Carolina 27526
TELEPHONE:	(919) 552-3782; (866) 552-3782
E-MAIL:	jbyrne@fuquayinn.com
WEBSITE:	www.fuquayinn.com
ROOMS:	3 Rooms; 1 Suite; 1 Carriage house; Private baths
CHILDREN:	Children age 12 and older welcome
ANIMALS:	Not allowed
HANDICAPPED:	Not handicapped accessible
DIETARY NEEDS:	Will accommodate guests' special dietary needs

Grilled Salmon with Warm Pineapple Salsa

Makes 10 Servings

Salmon:

2½	pounds fresh salmon fillet
1	teaspoon lime juice
1	tablespoon lemon juice
2	teaspoons minced shallots
2	teaspoons minced garlic
½	teaspoon black pepper

Pineapple salsa:

3½	tablespoons unsalted butter
2	tablespoons minced shallots
3	tablespoons minced peeled fresh ginger
2	teaspoons minced seeded jalapeño pepper
1¼	cups fresh squeezed orange juice
1¼	pounds fresh pineapple, peeled, cored and chopped into small dice (or 1 (20-ounce) can pineapple tidbits, drained)
½	teaspoon curry powder
1	tablespoon chopped fresh mint
1	tablespoon chopped fresh basil

For the salmon: Preheat grill. Cut salmon into 10 portions and sprinkle with lime and lemon juice, shallots, garlic and peppercorns. Let salmon marinate while preparing the salsa, then grill salmon until done to your taste. Serve immediately with warm salsa.

For the salsa: Melt butter in a skillet over medium heat. Add shallots, ginger and jalapeño. Cook just until aroma is released. Add orange juice and cook until reduced slightly. Lower heat to low, add pineapple, curry powder, mint and basil; stir to combine and warm gently (do not let it come to a boil).

Fruit Specialties & Beverages

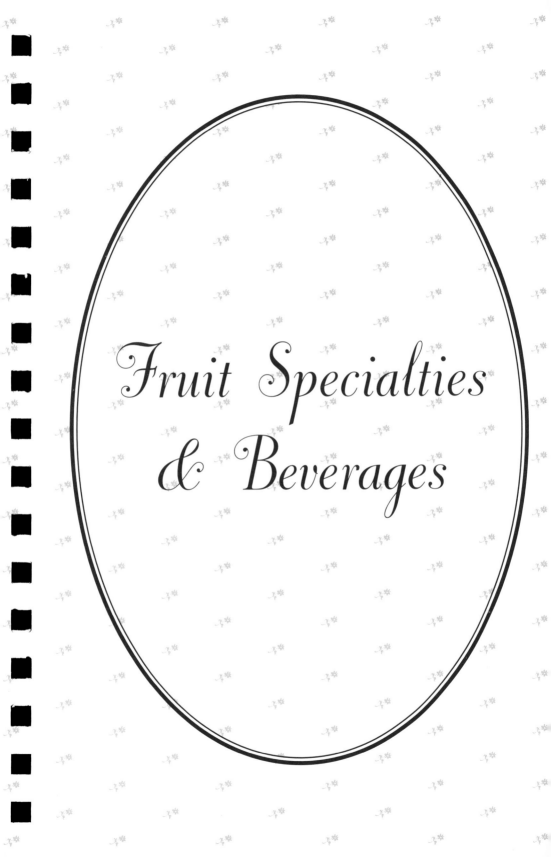

Fruit Specialties & Beverages

At Cumberland Falls Inn

At Cumberland Falls Inn is casual and elegant. Feel the richness of the original quilted maple woodwork which adorns the foyer. The living room has bay windows and ten-foot ceilings – you could describe this room as eclectic, from the camel leather sofa to the tapestry high-back chairs. Pick a book off the shelf and take a seat by the original wood-burning fireplace or enjoy the view of the gardens from the unique sunroom.

At Cumberland Falls Inn is located in the historic Montford district, three miles from the Biltmore Estate and close to all Asheville has to offer.

INNKEEPERS:	Patti & Gary Wiles
ADDRESS:	254 Cumberland Avenue
	Asheville, North Carolina 28801
TELEPHONE:	(888) 743-2557
E-MAIL:	fallsinn@aol.com
WEBSITE:	www.cumberlandfalls.com
ROOMS:	5 Rooms; Private baths
CHILDREN:	Children age 12 and older welcome
ANIMALS:	Not allowed
HANDICAPPED:	Not handicapped accessible
DIETARY NEEDS:	Will accommodate guests' special dietary needs

Peaches n' Cream

Makes 1 Serving

"This is used as a fruit dish. To say guests 'lap it up' is an understatement of its reception! Simply multiply the recipe as needed for the given number of guests."
~ Innkeeper, At Cumberland Falls Bed & Breakfast Inn

1	large ripe fresh peach, peeled, cut in half and pitted
½	tablespoon butter
2	teaspoons heavy cream
2	teaspoons white Zinfandel or other fruity white wine
½	teaspoon vanilla extract
1	tablespoon packed brown sugar

Pinch of cinnamon
Whipped cream, for serving

Preheat oven to 350°F. Clean peach cavity with a fruit baller. Put peach halves in a small baking dish. Put butter in cavity in each peach half. Add cream. Sprinkle wine over peach, letting some accumulate in bottom of dish. Sprinkle vanilla and brown sugar over peach. Sprinkle lightly with cinnamon. Bake for 20-30 minutes, until tender and bubbly. Serve with a dollop of whipped cream.

Owl's Nest Inn

The Owl's Nest Inn is located on 12 acres in the mountains just outside of Asheville and convenient to Great Smoky Mountains National Park, the Blue Ridge Parkway and hiking trails. This AAA Three Diamond and Mobil Three Star inn was built in 1885 and has been completely restored while maintaining its Victorian character.

The Engadine Suite is very private and romantic, with a spectacular view of the mountains. A queen-size canopy bed, soft robes and a whirlpool tub for two with an enclosed shower await your arrival.

INNKEEPERS:	Marg Dente & Gail Kinney
ADDRESS:	2630 Smokey Park Highway
	Candler, North Carolina 28715
TELEPHONE:	(828) 665-8325; (800) 665-8868
E-MAIL:	info@engadineinn.com
WEBSITE:	www.engadineinn.com
ROOMS:	5 Rooms; 1 Suite; 2 Cottages; Private baths
CHILDREN:	Children age 14 and older welcome
ANIMALS:	Not allowed; Resident dog & parrot
HANDICAPPED:	Not handicapped accessible
DIETARY NEEDS:	Will accommodate guests' special dietary needs

Engadine Inn
Breakfast Strawberries

Makes 4 to 5 Servings

"I created this recipe using strawberries gathered from the property that were first planted in 1885 for making strawberry wine. Plan ahead, this recipe needs to be started the night before." ~ Innkeeper, Owl's Nest Inn & Engadine Cabins

3	pints fresh strawberries, washed, stemmed and sliced
1	tablespoon sugar
¼	cup plus 2 tablespoons vanilla yogurt
½	teaspoon cinnamon
1½	teaspoons vanilla extract (or ¾ teaspoon vanilla extract plus ¾ teaspoon Grand Marnier)
4-5	mint leaves, for garnish

Combine strawberries and sugar; mix well. Cover and refrigerate overnight.

The next day, stir strawberries and divide among 4 or 5 attractive serving dishes. Combine yogurt, cinnamon and vanilla. Top strawberries with a dollop of yogurt mixture. Garnish with a mint leaf and serve.

Dry Ridge Inn

"Enchantment is a willingness
to live in a bungalow of stories,
rather than a warehouse
of facts."
~Thomas Moore

The Dry Ridge Inn is located "where life is as it should be." The inn is Weaverville's first bed & breakfast, opened by innkeepers with 19 years of experience as Asheville bed & breakfast owners. The inn offers a relaxed, small town ambiance in "a simpler time, a sweeter place," only 10 minutes from downtown Asheville and the Biltmore Estate. Enjoy Asheville, then come out to the country and the Dry Ridge Inn.

Remnants of the original homestead building and a hand-dug, stone-lined well still stand in the lower pasture, defiant of the passage of time.

INNKEEPERS:	Howard & Kristen Dusenbery
ADDRESS:	26 Brown Street
	Weaverville, North Carolina 28787
TELEPHONE:	(828) 658-3899; (800) 839-3899
E-MAIL:	innkeeper@dryridgeinn.com
WEBSITE:	www.dryridgeinn.com
ROOMS:	8 Rooms; Private baths
CHILDREN:	Welcome
ANIMALS:	Not allowed; Resident cats
HANDICAPPED:	Not handicapped accessible
DIETARY NEEDS:	Will accommodate guests' special dietary needs

Dry Ridge Inn Baked Apples

Makes 6 Servings

½   cup packed brown sugar
3   tablespoons butter
6   small apples, peeled and cored
Walnuts
Dried cherries
Cream or vanilla ice cream, for serving

Preheat oven to 350°F. Heat brown sugar and butter in a small saucepan over medium heat until sugar is melted and combined. Bring to a boil and boil for 1 minute, stirring constantly.

Put apples in a small baking dish. Fill center of each apple with walnuts and dried cherries. Pour brown sugar mixture over apples. Bake for 35 minutes, basting at least once. Serve with cream or ice cream.

Biltmore Village Inn

The official name of the Biltmore Village Inn is the Samuel Harrison Reed House. The house was among the first in Asheville to have running water and a bathroom. It was constructed in 1892 for Samuel Reed, the eldest son of Joseph and Katherine Miller Reed. Reed was the senior member of the law firm of Reed and Van Winkle.

In 1888, he sold a tract of land to George Washington Vanderbilt, which included the present Biltmore Village, but excluded the hilltop contiguous to the south of town, the site on which he built his house.

INNKEEPERS:	Ripley Hotch & Owen Sullivan
ADDRESS:	119 Dodge Street
	Asheville, North Carolina 28803
TELEPHONE:	(828) 274-8707; (866) 274-8779
E-MAIL:	info@biltmorevillageinn.com
WEBSITE:	www.biltmorevillageinn.com
ROOMS:	4 Rooms; 2 Suites; 1 Cottage; Private baths
CHILDREN:	Children age 12 and older welcome
ANIMALS:	Dogs under 45 pounds welcome; Resident dog
HANDICAPPED:	Not handicapped accessible
DIETARY NEEDS:	Will accommodate guests' special dietary needs

Caribbean Pears

Makes 8 Servings

"This dish always gets a lively reaction from guests." ~ Innkeeper, Biltmore Village Inn

4	pears, peeled, halved and cored
½	stick butter
1	cup packed brown sugar
1	cup orange juice
1	teaspoon coconut extract
3	cinnamon sticks, broken into "pear stem" lengths
1	kiwi, peeled, halved lengthwise and sliced

Preheat oven to 350°F. Put pears cut-side-down in a 7x11-inch baking dish. Heat butter and brown sugar in a saucepan over medium-low heat until melted and combined. Stir in orange juice and coconut extract. Bring mixture to a low boil, then pour over pears. Bake pears for 30 minutes.

Put 1 pear half on each plate. Pour a little pan sauce over each pear. Put a piece of cinnamon stick at the tip of each pear as a "stem," arrange kiwi around "stem" as "leaves" and serve.

The River Lodge

The River Lodge sits on six acres of manicured grounds with several streams that flow into the Tuckasegee River. A cascading waterfall runs along the side of the inn with a standing forest of 100-year-old pines as the backdrop. Sit on the porches and balconies and enjoy the river, waterfalls, streams and mountain views that surround you in this elegant retreat.

A special touch of flavors will awaken your taste buds at breakfast as you begin to plan the day's adventures – whether that's touring western North Carolina, hiking or shopping.

INNKEEPERS:	Cathy & Anthony Sgambato
ADDRESS:	619 Roy Tritt Road
	Cullowhee, North Carolina 28723
TELEPHONE:	(877) 384-4400
E-MAIL:	cathy@riverlodge-bb.com
WEBSITE:	www.riverlodge-bb.com
ROOMS:	5 Rooms; 1 Suite; Private baths
CHILDREN:	Children age 13 and older welcome
ANIMALS:	Not allowed; Resident dog
HANDICAPPED:	Not handicapped accessible
DIETARY NEEDS:	Will accommodate guests' special dietary needs

Breakfast Dessert Sundae

Makes 8 Servings

"A wonderful spring or summer breakfast dessert!" ~ Innkeeper, The River Lodge Bed & Breakfast

1	large cantaloupe
8	teaspoons maple syrup
8	tablespoons sour cream
8	teaspoons toasted wheat germ
8	medium strawberries, stems removed
32	blueberries

Cut cantaloupe in half, then cut each half into quarters, yielding 8 wedges. Remove rind and then cut each wedge into 8-10 pieces. Divide cantaloupe among 8 dessert bowls. Add 1 teaspoon of maple syrup to each bowl and stir cantaloupe to coat. Top with 1 tablespoon of sour cream. Sprinkle with 1 teaspoon of wheat germ. Slice strawberries vertically and place standing up in sour cream. Dot each bowl with 4 blueberries and serve.

The Cove

Welcome to beautiful Ocracoke, on the Outer Banks. After a relaxing ferry ride, the Cove Bed & Breakfast provides a quiet location for a great getaway. Start the day with a scrumptious breakfast, take one of the inn's bikes and spend hours exploring Ocracoke's seashore (ranked third on Dr. Beach's "America's Best Beaches 2004") and the village, paddle around in a kayak, go charter fishing in the Gulfstream or simply do nothing.

Stretch out and unwind. The inn's tastefully decorated rooms and suites offer a special setting for honeymoons, anniversaries or just a weekend away.

INNKEEPERS:	Jim and Mary Ellen Piland
ADDRESS:	21 Loop Road
	Ocracoke, North Carolina 27960
TELEPHONE:	(252) 928-4192
E-MAIL:	thecovebb@beachlink.com
WEBSITE:	www.thecovebb.com
ROOMS:	4 Rooms; 2 Suites; Private baths
CHILDREN:	Children age 15 and older welcome
ANIMALS:	Not allowed
HANDICAPPED:	Not handicapped accessible
DIETARY NEEDS:	Will accommodate guests' special dietary needs

Pineapple Breakfast Dessert

Makes 6 to 8 Servings

"When we serve our pineapple breakfast dessert, our guests pass on extra biscuits to leave room for more pineapple!" ~ Innkeeper, The Cove Bed & Breakfast

2	(20-ounce) cans pineapple (tidbits, crushed or chunks), drained
1	cup grated extra-sharp cheddar cheese
1	cup sugar
¼	cup all-purpose flour
1	sleeve Ritz crackers, crushed
1	stick butter, melted

Preheat oven to 350°F. Grease a 9x13-inch baking dish. Combine pineapple, cheese, sugar and flour; spread in a baking dish. Combine crackers and butter; sprinkle over pineapple mixture. Bake for 30 minutes. Serve warm.

1902 Turnpike House

This distinctly grand, circa 1902 home has seen a lot of history in the high country of the Blue Ridge Mountains. Rethink the cabin or cottage idea and reserve your quarters at the 1902 Turnpike House.

Begin your day with a freshly brewed cup of coffee on the expansive front porch before enjoying a breakfast feast served on fine china and heirloom crystal. Then explore the area and enjoy antique shopping, arts and crafts galleries, hiking, river rafting, horseback riding and golf, or visit Blowing Rock or Boone, both of which are about 30 minutes away.

INNKEEPERS:	Paul & Cindy Goedhart
ADDRESS:	317 Old Turnpike Road
	Banner Elk, North Carolina 28604
TELEPHONE:	(828) 898-5611; (888) 802-4487
E-MAIL:	info@1902turnpikehouse.com
WEBSITE:	www.1902turnpikehouse.com
ROOMS:	7 Rooms; Private baths
CHILDREN:	Children age 10 and older welcome
ANIMALS:	Not allowed; Resident dog
HANDICAPPED:	Not handicapped accessible
DIETARY NEEDS:	Will accommodate guests' special dietary needs

Aunt Laurie's Apple Crisp

Makes 10 to 12 Servings

*"A family favorite that has become a tradition at our inn." ~ Innkeeper, 1902
Turnpike House Bed & Breakfast*

2	tablespoons butter, softened plus 1½ sticks butter, melted
4	cups chopped peeled apples (Braeburns work best)
1	cup white sugar
3	tablespoons mini tapioca pearls (regular or minute)
¾	cup packed brown sugar
¾	cup all-purpose flour
¾	cup quick-cooking oats

Preheat oven to 350°F. Butter an 8x8-inch baking pan with the 2 tablespoons
of butter. In a large bowl, combine apples, white sugar and tapioca; spread
over bottom of pan. In a medium bowl, combine brown sugar, flour, oats
and the 1½ sticks of melted butter; spread over apples, pressing firmly. Bake
for 35 minutes, or until topping is browned and apples are bubbly.

Big Mill

The Big Mill Bed & Breakfast sits amid acres of farmland and forest in the quiet coastal plain of eastern North Carolina. About two hours from Raleigh-Durham and Norfolk, the inn is set in a lush landscape where streams and rivers meander through cypress swamps and fertile farmland.

With over 200 acres of grounds, you can wander through the landscaped gardens, explore the original farm outbuildings or walk through woodlands. Shaded by stately, 89-year-old pecan trees planted by the owner's parents, the house has been in the innkeeper's family since 1920.

INNKEEPERS:	Chloe G. Tuttle
ADDRESS:	1607 Big Mill Road
	Williamston, North Carolina 27892
TELEPHONE:	(252) 792-8787
E-MAIL:	info@bigmill.com
WEBSITE:	www.bigmill.com
ROOMS:	2 Rooms; 2 Suites; Private baths
CHILDREN:	Children age 10 and older welcome
ANIMALS:	Not allowed; Resident outdoor cat
HANDICAPPED:	Not handicapped accessible
DIETARY NEEDS:	Will accommodate guests' special dietary needs

Ginger Pineapple Spread

Makes 1 Cup

"Serve this spread with quick breads, such as cranberry bread, pumpkin bread, yellow squash bread, etc." ~ Innkeeper, Big Mill Bed & Breakfast

1   (8-ounce) container pineapple cream cheese, softened
1   tablespoon calamondin, kumquat or orange marmalade*
Grated zest of 1 orange
1   teaspoon finely chopped crystallized (candied) ginger
Cranberry, pumpkin, yellow squash or other quick bread, for serving

Beat cream cheese, marmalade, orange zest and ginger with a mixer on medium speed for several minutes, until thoroughly combined. Chill, then serve with sliced quick bread.

*Note: A calamondin, also known as a Panama orange or Scarlet or Golden lime, is a small citrus fruit resembling a miniature tangerine. They are very juicy, with a sweet but acidic flavor.

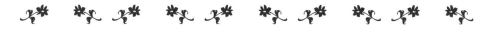

Lodges on Lake Lure

T he Lodge on Lake Lure is located in Hickory Nut Gorge, one of the most beautiful canyons in the eastern United States. The gorge is about 14 miles long, and extends from the small village of Gerton through Bat Cave and Chimney Rock to Lake Lure. The rushing Rocky Broad River flows through the gorge and empties into the crystal waters of the lake.

Guest rooms are decorated with charming country antiques and many have terraces or balconies overlooking the lake. A lavish full breakfast and evening wine and hors d'oeuvres are offered each day.

INNKEEPERS:	Gisela Hopke
ADDRESS:	361 Charlotte Drive
	Lake Lure, North Carolina 28746
TELEPHONE:	(828) 625-2789; (800) 733-2785
E-MAIL:	info@lodgeonlakelure.com
WEBSITE:	www.lodgeonlakelure.com
ROOMS:	17 Rooms; Private baths
CHILDREN:	Children age 8 and older welcome
ANIMALS:	Not allowed; Resident cat
HANDICAPPED:	Handicapped accessible
DIETARY NEEDS:	Will accommodate guests' special dietary needs

North Carolina Apple Chutney

Makes 4 Cups

1   medium red onion, diced
Zest and juice of 1 orange
1   teaspoon dried thyme
1   bay leaf
4   North Carolina Gala apples, peeled, cored and diced
1   teaspoon cinnamon
¼   cup dried cranberries
¼   cup currants
¼   cup golden raisins
¼   cup plus 2 tablespoons champagne vinegar
½   cup clover honey
¼   cup fresh lemon juice
1   cup chopped walnuts, toasted

Combine onion, orange zest, thyme and bay leaf in a skillet over medium heat; cook, stirring frequently, for 8-10 minutes, until onions are soft. Stir in apples, cinnamon, dried cranberries, currants and raisins; cook for 3 minutes. Stir in vinegar, honey and orange and lemon juices; cook for 5 minutes. Stir in walnuts. Serve warm over pork or chicken.

Note: This chutney may be made several days in advance, covered and refrigerated. Reheat the chutney when ready to serve.

Lamplight Inn

Located 45 minutes from the Raleigh-Durham airport, the Lamplight Inn sits on a 150-year-old, five-acre tobacco farm. Let the innkeeper beckon you with the soft glow of the many chimney lamps used to light this restored farm. Relax on the wrap-around porch or stroll the grounds.

A short drive will bring you to the Kerr Lake State Recreation Area to enjoy sailing, fishing, water skiing and hiking on a 50,000-acre, man-made lake. More than 800 miles of wooded shoreline provide access to a variety of fun-filled activities.

INNKEEPERS:	Shirley Payne
ADDRESS:	1680 Flemingtown Road
	Henderson, North Carolina 27537
TELEPHONE:	(252) 438-6311; (877) 222-0100
E-MAIL:	inn@lamplightbandb.com
WEBSITE:	www.lamplightbandb.com
ROOMS:	4 Rooms; Private baths
CHILDREN:	Welcome
ANIMALS:	Call ahead
HANDICAPPED:	Handicapped accessible
DIETARY NEEDS:	Will accommodate guests' special dietary needs

Cranberry Chutney

Makes 5 to 6 Cups

"Cranberries never tasted so good – this recipe always gets rave reviews." –
Innkeeper, Lamplight Inn

1	cup chopped peeled orange
¼	cup orange juice
4	cups fresh or frozen cranberries
2	cups sugar
½	cup raisins
1	cup chopped unpeeled apple
½	teaspoon cinnamon
½	teaspoon ground ginger
1	tablespoon apple cider vinegar
½	cup chopped nuts

Combine all ingredients in a large saucepan over medium-high heat. Bring
to a boil, lower heat and simmer for 10 minutes, or until cranberries burst.
Chill until serving.

Inn on Main Street

The innkeepers at the Inn on Main Street bring casual hospitality to a century-old Victorian bed & breakfast furnished with lovely antiques. This romantic AAA Three Diamond inn is located just ten minutes from Asheville, 15 minutes from the Biltmore Estate and a short, scenic drive below Bull Gap on the Blue Ridge Parkway. Also nearby are whitewater rafting, skiing, golf, trail rides and the mineral baths at Hot Springs Spa.

Quaint, quiet Weaverville is home to arts and crafts studios, art galleries, the Milling Company restaurant and Zebulon Vance's birthplace.

INNKEEPERS:	Dan & Nancy Ward
ADDRESS:	88 South Main Street
	Weaverville, North Carolina 28787
TELEPHONE:	(828) 645-4935; (877) 873-6074
E-MAIL:	relax@innonmain.com
WEBSITE:	www.innonmain.com
ROOMS:	7 Rooms; Private baths
CHILDREN:	Children age 12 and older welcome
ANIMALS:	Not allowed; Resident outdoor dog
HANDICAPPED:	Not handicapped accessible
DIETARY NEEDS:	Will accommodate guests' special dietary needs

Mango Salsa

Makes 2 Cups

"Serve this salsa with tortilla chips, grilled fish or your favorite Mexican dish."
~ Innkeeper, Inn on Main Street

2   mangoes, peeled and diced
1   jalapeño pepper, seeded and minced
2   tablespoons minced red bell pepper
Juice of 1 lime
¼   sweet onion, diced
1   teaspoon salt
3   tablespoons chopped cilantro
½   teaspoon cumin

Combine all ingredients, chill and serve.

Big Mill

The Big Mill sits amid acres of farmland and forest in the quiet coastal plain of eastern North Carolina. This is a lush landscape where streams and rivers meander through cypress swamps and fertile farmland.

A delicious continental breakfast is served in your room and consists of homemade sourdough or sweet breads made with fruits and nuts grown on the farm. Grapes, plums, pears and blueberries from the orchard are served in season. Crustless quiches made with dried tomatoes from the cook's garden and homemade yogurt are favorites.

INNKEEPERS:	Chloe G. Tuttle
ADDRESS:	1607 Big Mill Road
	Williamston, North Carolina 27892
TELEPHONE:	(252) 792-8787
E-MAIL:	info@bigmill.com
WEBSITE:	www.bigmill.com
ROOMS:	2 Rooms; 2 Suites; Private baths
CHILDREN:	Children age 10 and older welcome
ANIMALS:	Not allowed; Resident outdoor cat
HANDICAPPED:	Not handicapped accessible
DIETARY NEEDS:	Will accommodate guests' special dietary needs

Mulled Cider

Makes 8 Servings

"Serve hot on a cold day. This brew imparts a wonderful aroma in the house. It's also good with a dash of brandy or rum." ~ Innkeeper, Big Mill Bed & Breakfast

7-8 whole cloves
1   orange, washed
2   quarts apple cider
¼   cup light brown sugar
2   sticks cinnamon
⅛   teaspoon ground ginger (or 1 teaspoon minced fresh ginger)
½   lemon, washed and sliced

Stick cloves in orange, then slice orange. Put all ingredients in a soup pot or crock pot. Bring to a boil, lower heat to low and simmer for 30 minutes. Serve hot.

Desserts

Desserts

Bed & Breakfast at Ponder Cove

Come visit the Bed & Breakfast at Ponder Cove, the premier dog-friendly lodging in western North Carolina. Innkeeper Gary Rawlins was trained at England's leading furniture college for designer and makers. His work is heavily influenced by the traditions of England's greatest Arts and Crafts leaders of the past and its best contemporary furniture makers.

Gary's work has won numerous awards and he has been featured in *Fine Woodworking Magazine.* He counts movie director Barry Levinson and cartoonist Charles Shultz among his clients.

INNKEEPERS:	Martha Abraham & Gary Rawlins
ADDRESS:	1067 Ponder Creek Road
	Mars Hill, North Carolina 28754
TELEPHONE:	(828) 689-7304; (866) 689-7304
E-MAIL:	martha@ponder.com
WEBSITE:	www.pondercove.com
ROOMS:	3 Suites; Private baths
CHILDREN:	Call ahead
ANIMALS:	Dogs welcome; Resident dogs
HANDICAPPED:	Not handicapped accessible
DIETARY NEEDS:	Will accommodate guests' special dietary needs

Martha's Toffee Oatmeal Cookies

Makes 36 Cookies

1½ cups all-purpose flour
1 teaspoon baking soda
2 sticks unsalted butter, softened
¾ cup white sugar
¾ cup packed brown sugar
1 egg
1 teaspoon vanilla extract
1½ cups old-fashioned rolled oats
1 cup dried cherries, Craisins or dried cranberries
1 cup coarsely chopped bittersweet chocolate
1 cup toffee pieces

Preheat oven to 350°F. Sift together flour and baking soda into a small bowl. In a large bowl, with a mixer on medium speed, beat butter and white and brown sugars for 2-3 minutes, until light and fluffy. Beat in egg on high speed. Beat in vanilla. Beat in flour mixture on low speed, a little at a time, until well combined. Stir in oats, dried cherries, chocolate and toffee by hand.

Divide dough into 3 pieces and, using plastic wrap, roll into approximately 1½-inch-diameter logs. Cut each log into ¾-inch-thick slices and bake on a parchment paper-lined baking sheet for 8-10 minutes, until golden brown. Remove from oven and transfer to a wire rack to cool.

Note: These cookies can be baked immediately, refrigerated for 1-2 days or frozen for up to a month. Do a few at a time when you can't resist. Yum!

Carol's Garden Inn

Come stay at Durham's most relaxing bed & breakfast inn. This circa 1910 home has been completely renovated to take you back to a bygone era of Southern hospitality. You can relax on the deck and watch the colorful fish in the water garden, sit by the large lower pond, stroll the grounds or restore your soul in your beautifully decorated, spacious, quiet bedroom with private bath and whirlpool tub.

The comfortable bed will restore your body and the quiet solitude will heal your soul. In the morning, enjoy a great breakfast to start your day.

INNKEEPERS:	Carol & Steve Barden
ADDRESS:	2412 South Alston Avenue
	Durham, North Carolina 27713
TELEPHONE:	(919) 680-6777; (877) 922-6777
E-MAIL:	carol@carolsgardeninn.com
WEBSITE:	www.carolsgardeninn.com
ROOMS:	2 Rooms; Private baths
CHILDREN:	Children age 10 and older welcome
ANIMALS:	Not allowed
HANDICAPPED:	Not handicapped accessible
DIETARY NEEDS:	Will accommodate guests' special dietary needs

German Crunch Cookies

Makes 48 Cookies

"This recipe is adapted from one of my father's. He was a baker for 50 years."
~ Innkeeper, Carol's Garden Inn

1½	sticks butter, softened
¾	cup white sugar
1	cup plus 2 tablespoons packed brown sugar
1	teaspoon vanilla extract
2	eggs
2	cups all-purpose flour
1	cup quick-cooking oats
1	teaspoon salt
1	teaspoon baking soda
1½	cups chopped walnuts

Preheat oven to 370°F. In a large bowl, beat butter, white and brown sugars and vanilla until creamy. Add eggs and mix well. In a small bowl, mix flour, oats, salt and baking soda; stir into butter mixture. Stir in nuts. Drop dough by teaspoonsful onto an ungreased baking sheet. Bake for 10 minutes.

Old North Durham Inn

G uests of the Old North Durham Inn are invited to enjoy the hospitality of this restored, early 1900 Colonial Revival home. The rocker-lined wrap-around porch is a perfect place to enjoy an early morning cup of coffee or a homemade afternoon treat from the always-stocked cookie jar.

Warm hospitality and personal service are key elements of this inn's success. As one guest commented, "It truly seems like another world that you have created. Everything about your inn speaks 'welcome weary traveler – enter and find rest.'"

INNKEEPERS:	Debbie & Jim Vickery
ADDRESS:	922 North Mangum Street
	Durham, North Carolina 27701
TELEPHONE:	(919) 683-1885
E-MAIL:	dvick1885@aol.com
WEBSITE:	www.bbonline.com/nc/oldnorth
ROOMS:	3 Rooms; 1 Suite; Private baths
CHILDREN:	Welcome
ANIMALS:	Not allowed; Resident dog
HANDICAPPED:	Not handicapped accessible
DIETARY NEEDS:	Will accommodate guests' special dietary needs

Phyllis' Ginger Cookies

Makes About 48 Cookies

"These cookies are a staple of my husband's family in Maine. They come out so round and perfect that guests think they are store-bought … until they bite into them!" ~ Innkeeper, Old North Durham Inn

¼	cup plus 2 tablespoons vegetable shortening
½	stick plus 2 tablespoons margarine or butter, softened
1	cup sugar
1	egg, beaten
¼	cup molasses
2	cups unsifted all-purpose flour
1	tablespoon baking soda
½	teaspoon salt
1	teaspoon cinnamon
1	teaspoon ground cloves
1	teaspoon ground ginger

Preheat oven to 350°F. Cream together shortening, margarine, sugar, egg and molasses. Stir in flour, baking soda, salt, cinnamon, cloves and ginger. Roll dough into 1-inch balls. Bake on an ungreased cookie sheet for 12-15 minutes (cookies should be crinkly and soft on top when done).

803 Elizabeth

E ach morning, a continental breakfast featuring homemade muffin tops, fresh fruit, juice and cereal is served in the dining room or, weather permitting, on one of the porches. Special attention is given to healthful breakfasts. Upon request, the innkeepers can provide a full breakfast and can accommodate vegetarian or other special diet options.

The three guest rooms at 803 Elizabeth are furnished with family antiques, ironed linens and cut flowers from the garden.

INNKEEPERS:	Martha & Will Krauss
ADDRESS:	803 Elizabeth Lane
	Matthews, North Carolina 28105
TELEPHONE:	(704) 841-8900; (800) 327-4843
E-MAIL:	mwkrauss@carolina.rr.com
WEBSITE:	www.803elizabeth.com
ROOMS:	3 Rooms; Private baths
CHILDREN:	Children age 6 and older welcome
ANIMALS:	Not allowed
HANDICAPPED:	Not handicapped accessible
DIETARY NEEDS:	Will accommodate guests' special dietary needs

Toasted Coconut Cookies

Makes 36 Cookies

"This cookie recipe is from a friend in yoga class." ~ Innkeeper, 803 Elizabeth Bed & Breakfast

1	cup sweetened flaked coconut
1	stick butter, softened
¾	cup sugar
1	large egg
½	teaspoon coconut or almond extract
1½	cups all-purpose flour
½	teaspoon baking soda
1	teaspoon baking powder
½	cup crispy rice cereal
½	cup old-fashioned rolled oats

Preheat oven to 350°F. Spread coconut on a baking sheet and toast lightly in oven for 7-10 minutes; remove from oven and cool.

In a large bowl, beat butter until fluffy. Gradually beat in sugar. Add egg and coconut or almond extract; beat well. In a medium bowl, combine flour, baking soda and baking powder. Add flour mixture to butter mixture, a little at a time, beating well after each addition. Stir in coconut, crispy rice cereal and oats.

Drop dough by heaping teaspoonful onto a parchment paper-lined cookie sheet. (The cookie sheet can be greased instead, but parchment paper makes cookie baking much easier – no cookie sheets to wash!) Bake cookies for 12-15 minutes, until golden. Slide parchment paper off cookie sheet and let cookies cool.

Turn of the Century Victorian

T he circa 1905 Heilig-Dees home is one of the finest examples of late Victorian architecture in Salisbury's West Square Historic District. Purchased in 1997 by innkeeper Karen Windate, the home underwent a painstaking, two-year historic restoration.

This is the second home Karen has lovingly restored to its original splendor. The first was an 1890s Victorian in the historic district of Madison, Georgia. The Heilig-Dees restoration has won praise from the historic preservation community, the city of Salisbury and the inn's pampered guests.

INNKEEPERS:	Karen Windate
ADDRESS:	259 South Fulton Street
	Salisbury, North Carolina 28144
TELEPHONE:	(704) 642-1660; (800) 250-5349
E-MAIL:	info@turnofthecenturybb.com
WEBSITE:	www.turnofthecenturybb.com
ROOMS:	3 Rooms; 1 Suite; Private baths
CHILDREN:	Children age 12 and older welcome
ANIMALS:	Not allowed
HANDICAPPED:	Not handicapped accessible
DIETARY NEEDS:	Will accommodate guests' special dietary needs

Soft Sour Cream Sugar Cookies

Makes About 30 Cookies

"This was one of my grandmother's favorite cookies. The sour cream flavor is a nice addition to the wonderful, soft sugar cookie." ~ Innkeeper, Turn of the Century Victorian Bed & Breakfast

½	cup shortening or 1 stick butter, softened
1	cup plus 1 tablespoon sugar
2	eggs
2	cups all-purpose flour
1	teaspoon salt
½	teaspoon baking soda
2	teaspoons baking powder
½	cup sour cream
½	teaspoon vanilla extract
¼	teaspoon cinnamon

Preheat oven to 400°F. In a large bowl, cream shortening and 1 cup of sugar. Add eggs, 1 at a time, beating well after each addition. Sift together flour, salt, baking soda and baking powder into a medium bowl. In a small bowl, mix sour cream and vanilla. Add flour and sour cream mixtures alternately to shortening mixture, stirring after each addition and ending with flour mixture (do not overmix).

Drop batter by teaspoonsful onto a parchment paper-lined or greased cookie sheet. Combine remaining 1 tablespoon of sugar and cinnamon; sprinkle over cookies. Bake for 10 minutes.

The Moss House

The Moss House was built by Frank Adams Moss and Mary Bonner Moss shortly after their marriage in 1898. Construction started in 1900 and was completed in 1902. Local timber, milled at the Moss Planing Mill, provided much of the lumber. The hardwood floors are heart pine. The carved mantles, each unique in design, were milled especially for the house, and three of the four guestrooms feature their original mantles.

Family heirlooms, antiques and collectibles lend the interior an atmosphere of ease and grace, with a flair for the Caribbean.

INNKEEPERS:	Mary Havens Cooper
ADDRESS:	129 Van Norden Street
	Washington, North Carolina 27889
TELEPHONE:	(252) 975-3967; (888) 975-3393
E-MAIL:	info@themosshouse.com
WEBSITE:	www.themosshouse.com
ROOMS:	4 Rooms; 1 Suite; Private baths
CHILDREN:	Children age 6 and older welcome
ANIMALS:	Not allowed
HANDICAPPED:	Not handicapped accessible
DIETARY NEEDS:	Will accommodate guests' special dietary needs

Duncan Hines Chocolate Chip Cookies

Makes About 36 Cookies

"These cookies were made for me by my childhood sweetheart and I'm still making them 30 years later." ~ Innkeeper, The Moss House Bed & Breakfast

1	(10½-ounce) package Duncan Hines Deluxe II white cake mix
¼	cup packed light brown sugar
1	cup semi-sweet chocolate chips
½	cup chopped nuts
¾	cup oil
1	egg

Preheat oven to 375°F. In a large bowl, mix all ingredients well. Drop dough by teaspoonful onto an ungreased cookie sheet. Bake for 10-12 minutes, until centers of cookies are golden brown (edges will look darker). Cool cookies on cookie sheet for about 1 minute, then remove to a wire rack and finish cooling.

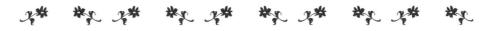

Corner Oak Manor

The Corner Oak Manor Bed & Breakfast is a circa 1920 English Tudor home situated in a quiet neighborhood just a half mile from the historic Biltmore House. Come nurture your senses in this comfortably elegant home. Your hosts will make you feel welcome and pampered. At Corner Oak Manor, you'll find sumptuous gourmet breakfasts, a refreshing Jacuzzi and gracious amenities in a relaxed ambiance.

If you want extra privacy, the cottage is the place for you! It has a living room/kitchen area with elaborately stenciled walls and a gas fireplace.

INNKEEPERS:	Karen & Andy Spradley
ADDRESS:	53 Saint Dunstans Road
	Asheville, North Carolina 28803
TELEPHONE:	(828) 253-3525; (888) 633-3525
E-MAIL:	info@corneroakmanor.com
WEBSITE:	www.corneroakmanor.com
ROOMS:	3 Rooms; 1 Cottage; Private baths
CHILDREN:	Children age 12 and older welcome
ANIMALS:	Not allowed
HANDICAPPED:	Not handicapped accessible
DIETARY NEEDS:	Will accommodate guests' special dietary needs

Double Chocolate Cherry Biscotti

Makes 36 Biscotti

2   tablespoons raspberry liqueur, warmed
1   cup dried cherries
2   cups all-purpose flour
1½ teaspoons baking powder
¼   teaspoon salt
¾   cup sugar
1   stick butter, softened
2   large eggs
2   ounces bittersweet chocolate, chopped into ¼-inch pieces
2   ounces white chocolate, chopped into ¼-inch pieces

Combine raspberry liqueur and cherries. Let stand for 30 minutes, then remove cherries and drain on paper towels; discard liqueur.

Preheat oven to 325°F. Sift together flour, baking powder and salt into a medium bowl. In a large bowl, with a mixer, beat sugar and butter for 2 minutes; scrape sides of bowl and beat for 4 minutes more, until very smooth. Add eggs, 1 at a time, beating after each addition and scraping bowl as needed. Beat on high speed for 30 seconds after eggs have been added. On low speed, slowly beat in flour mixture. Stir in chocolate and cherries by hand, mixing just to combine (a rubber spatula works well).

Turn dough out onto a floured surface and knead lightly. Divide dough into 2 pieces. Shape each piece into a 10-inch-long, 2-inch-wide and 1½-inch-thick log. Put logs on greased and floured or parchment paper-lined baking sheets. Bake for 35 minutes, rotating baking sheets after 18 minutes, until biscotti are just getting golden and are set. Remove from oven and let stand for at least 20 minutes. Transfer to a cutting board and cut diagonally into ½-inch-thick slices with a serrated knife. Stand biscotti upright on baking sheet and bake for 15-20 minutes more, or until dried through. Cool completely, then store in an airtight plastic container.

Note: The dough can be shaped into logs on the baking sheets. For lighter-looking biscotti, use all white chocolate.

William Thomas House

Welcome to the William Thomas House, where deluxe accommodations and finely appointed surroundings await you. The inn is located in the heart of downtown Raleigh, within walking distance of the governor's mansion, the capitol, museums, shopping, restaurants and more.

Prior to opening the inn, innkeeper Jim Lofton served as chief of staff for Jim Martin during his six terms in Congress and his two terms as governor of North Carolina. Innkeeper Sarah Lofton served as executive assistant to North Carolina's first lady Dottie Martin from 1985-1993.

INNKEEPERS:	Jim & Sarah Lofton
ADDRESS:	530 North Blount Street
	Raleigh, North Carolina 27604
TELEPHONE:	(919) 755-9400; (800) 653-3466
E-MAIL:	lofton@williamthomashouse.com
WEBSITE:	www.williamthomashouse.com
ROOMS:	4 Rooms; Private baths
CHILDREN:	Welcome
ANIMALS:	Not allowed
HANDICAPPED:	Not handicapped accessible
DIETARY NEEDS:	Will accommodate guests' special dietary needs

Coconut Pound Cake

Makes 1 Cake

3   sticks butter, softened
3   cups sugar
6   large eggs
1   (8-ounce) carton sour cream
3   cups all-purpose flour, sifted
1   cup coconut
1   tablespoon coconut flavoring

Preheat oven to 350°F. Grease and flour a tube cake pan. Cream together butter and sugar. Add eggs, 1 at a time, beating well after each addition. Add sour cream and flour alternately, ⅓ at a time, mixing well after each addition. Stir in coconut and coconut flavoring. Pour batter into pan. Bake for 80 minutes, or until a toothpick inserted in center comes out clean.

Biltmore Village Inn

The Biltmore Village Inn is housed in a fully restored 1892 Queen Anne Victorian. Elegant in design, handsome in its museum-quality collections and furnished with every comfort, the Biltmore Village Inn will fulfill your idea of what an inn should be.

This is the innkeepers' third bed & breakfast inn, and they have included all the amenities guests have asked for over the years. The unusually large bedrooms and baths have whirlpool tubs and fireplaces. A gourmet breakfast and afternoon tea offer a great beginning and end to the day.

INNKEEPERS:	Ripley Hotch & Owen Sullivan
ADDRESS:	119 Dodge Street
	Asheville, North Carolina 28803
TELEPHONE:	(828) 274-8707; (866) 274-8779
E-MAIL:	info@biltmorevillageinn.com
WEBSITE:	www.biltmorevillageinn.com
ROOMS:	4 Rooms; 2 Suites; 1 Cottage; Private baths
CHILDREN:	Children age 12 and older welcome
ANIMALS:	Dogs under 45 pounds welcome; Resident dog
HANDICAPPED:	Not handicapped accessible
DIETARY NEEDS:	Will accommodate guests' special dietary needs

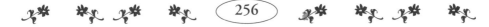

Cold Oven Pound Cake

Makes 1 Cake

"This pound cake has a wonderful texture and a delightful, sugary crust. Plan ahead, it should sit for a day before slicing. This cake freezes beautifully." ~ Innkeeper, Biltmore Village Inn

2	sticks butter, softened
½	cup vegetable oil
4	eggs
3	cups all-purpose flour
¼	teaspoon salt
3	cups sugar
1	cup milk
½	teaspoon rum extract
1	teaspoon vanilla extract
1	teaspoon lemon extract

Grease a large tube cake pan. In a large bowl, beat butter and oil until smooth. Add eggs, 1 at a time, beating well after each addition. In a medium bowl, combine flour, salt and sugar. Add flour mixture and milk alternately to butter mixture, mixing well after each addition. Add rum, vanilla and lemon extracts; mix well. Pour batter into pan. Place pan in a cold oven. Turn oven temperature to 350°F and bake for 90 minutes.

Variations: Soak 1 cup of raisins in ½ cup of brandy, drain and toss with ½ cup flour. Stir raisins into batter last. Add your favorite nuts with or instead of the raisins.

Hanna House

The Hanna House is located in New Bern, North Carolina's second oldest town, founded in 1710 by a Swiss nobleman who named it after his native city of Berne, Switzerland. The town is a historic treasure with more than 150 buildings listed as contributing to its designation as a National Register Historic District.

The innkeepers pride themselves in presenting unique, gourmet breakfasts. A sample menu might include nectarine crumble, eggs Florentine with homemade English muffins, yam hash browns and thick-sliced bacon.

INNKEEPERS:	Camille & Joe Klotz
ADDRESS:	218 Pollock Street
	New Bern, North Carolina 28560
TELEPHONE:	(252) 635-3209; (866) 830-4371
E-MAIL:	hannahouse@lpmonline.net
WEBSITE:	www.hannahousenc.net
ROOMS:	2 Rooms; 1 Suite; Private baths
CHILDREN:	Children age 12 and older welcome
ANIMALS:	Not allowed; Resident dog
HANDICAPPED:	Not handicapped accessible
DIETARY NEEDS:	Will accommodate guests' special dietary needs

Old-Fashioned Marble Cake

Makes 12 Servings

Dark part:

2¼	cups all-purpose flour, sifted
1	teaspoon baking soda
⅜	teaspoon salt
1½	teaspoons cinnamon
1	teaspoon ground cloves
1½	sticks butter, softened
¾	cup packed dark brown sugar
3	egg yolks, beaten
3	tablespoons molasses
¾	cup buttermilk

Light part:

2	cups cake flour, sifted
1	teaspoon baking powder
1	teaspoon baking soda
⅜	teaspoon salt
5⅓	tablespoons butter
1	teaspoon vanilla extract
¾	cup sugar, divided
¾	cup buttermilk
3	egg whites

For the dark part: Preheat oven to 350°F. Line bottom and 3½-inches up sides of a 9-inch tube pan with parchment paper. Sift together flour, baking soda, salt, cinnamon and cloves 3 times. Cream butter. Slowly add brown sugar, creaming well. Stir in egg yolks, then molasses; beat until fluffy. Add flour mixture and buttermilk alternately in 4-5 portions, starting and ending with flour and beating well after each addition.

For the light part: Sift together flour, baking powder, baking soda and salt 3 times. Cream butter. Add vanilla and ½ cup of sugar; mix well. Add flour mixture and buttermilk alternately in 4-5 portions, starting and ending with flour and beating well after each addition. Beat egg whites to a soft foam. Add remaining ¼ cup of sugar and beat egg whites until stiff; fold into batter. For a marbled effect, alternately spoon light and dark batter into pan. Bake for 1 hour, or until nicely browned. Cool in pan on a wire rack for 10 minutes, then carefully turn out onto rack and cool completely.

Maxwell House

Come stay in the Maxwell House, a 1901 Victorian home located in the foothills of the Blue Ridge Mountains and the Wine Country. The Maxwell House is located in Mt. Airy, home to Andy Griffith and Donna Fargo. Mayberry Days are celebrated in September. In October, come for the Autumn Leaves Festival and celebrate the spectacular fall colors.

When staying at the Maxwell House, you will not leave the table hungry or be in want of a thing until dinner time. Breakfast includes scones, muffins, quiches, stratas and fresh seasonal fruit and juices.

INNKEEPERS:	Twyla & Roger Sickmiller
ADDRESS:	618 North Main Street
	Mt. Airy, North Carolina 27030
TELEPHONE:	(336) 786-2174; (877) 786-2174
E-MAIL:	maxwellhousebb@hotmail.com
WEBSITE:	www.bbonline.com/nc/maxwellhouse
ROOMS:	4 Rooms; Private baths
CHILDREN:	Children age 12 and older welcome
ANIMALS:	Not allowed
HANDICAPPED:	Handicapped accessible; 1 room
DIETARY NEEDS:	Will accommodate guests' special dietary needs

Applesauce Cake

Makes 1 Cake

2	cups all-purpose flour
1	cup sugar
1	teaspoon cinnamon
½	teaspoon mace or nutmeg
¼	teaspoon ground cloves
2	teaspoons baking soda
1	cup raisins
1	cup chopped walnuts
1½	cups applesauce
1	teaspoon salt
1	stick butter, melted

Preheat oven to 350°F. Grease a 9x9-inch or 7x11-inch baking pan. Mix all ingredients until well combined. Pour batter into a pan. Bake for 45-50 minutes, or until a toothpick inserted in center comes out clean.

The Waverly Inn

The Waverly Inn offers breath-taking scenery, a year-round temperate climate, cultural pursuits and hospitality as it was meant to be. Recently renovated and listed on the National Register of Historic Places, the Waverly is Hendersonville's oldest inn. Cited in national publications such as *The New York Times* and *Southern Living*, the Waverly received high praise in *Vogue* magazine for its "massive Southern breakfast."

The innkeepers want to make everyone feel right at home. Join them each evening for a social hour with a favorite beverage and hors d'oeuvres.

INNKEEPERS:	John & Diane Sheiry and Darla Olmstead
ADDRESS:	783 Main Street
	Hendersonville, North Carolina 28792
TELEPHONE:	(828) 693-9193; (800) 537-8195
E-MAIL:	info@waverlyinn.com
WEBSITE:	www.waverlyinn.com
ROOMS:	13 Rooms; 1 Suite; Private baths
CHILDREN:	Welcome
ANIMALS:	Not allowed
HANDICAPPED:	Not handicapped accessible
DIETARY NEEDS:	Will accommodate guests' special dietary needs

Apple Cake

Makes 12 Servings

Raw sugar (natural sugar)
1½ cups all-purpose flour
1 cup packed brown sugar
1 teaspoon cinnamon
½ teaspoon nutmeg
1 teaspoon salt
1 teaspoon baking soda
1 teaspoon baking powder
1 stick butter, melted and cooled
½ cup vegetable oil
3 large eggs
¾ cup orange juice
Powdered sugar, for garnish (optional)

Apple topping:
1 large Granny Smith apple, thinly sliced
1 stick butter, melted and cooled
1 teaspoon cinnamon
¼ cup all-purpose flour

Preheat oven to 350°F. Spray a Bundt pan with non-stick cooking spray and sprinkle with raw sugar. In a large bowl, combine flour, brown sugar, cinnamon, nutmeg, salt, baking soda and baking powder. In a medium bowl, combine butter, oil, eggs and orange juice; add to flour mixture and stir to combine. Pour batter into pan. Arrange apple topping over batter. Bake for 40-45 minutes, or until a toothpick inserted in center comes out clean. Cool cake, then dust with powdered sugar, if desired.

For the apple topping: In a small bowl, combine apples, butter, cinnamon and flour; toss to coat apples well.

Hanna House

Welcome to the Hanna House Bed & Breakfast. Recently renovated and furnished with the finest antiques and Oriental carpets, the former Rudolph Ulrich House was built in 1896 by a successful New Bern grocer. The house has undergone periods of use and revival, the most recent attending to its turn-of-the-century details and creating a serene environment that encourages relaxation.

Designated as a historic home, the inn is steps away from all major local attractions and the confluence of the Neuse and Trent rivers.

INNKEEPERS:	Camille & Joe Klotz
ADDRESS:	218 Pollock Street
	New Bern, North Carolina 28560
TELEPHONE:	(252) 635-3209; (866) 830-4371
E-MAIL:	hannahouse@lpmonline.net
WEBSITE:	www.hannahousenc.net
ROOMS:	2 Rooms; 1 Suite; Private baths
CHILDREN:	Children age 12 and older welcome
ANIMALS:	Not allowed; Resident dog
HANDICAPPED:	Not handicapped accessible
DIETARY NEEDS:	Will accommodate guests' special dietary needs

Sweet Potato Layer Cake

Makes 12 Servings

3 cups cake flour
2 teaspoons baking powder
2 teaspoons baking soda
2 teaspoons cinnamon
1 teaspoon ground ginger
½ teaspoon salt
¼ teaspoon ground cloves
1 cup vegetable oil
1 cup white sugar
1 cup packed light brown sugar
4 large eggs
2 cups mashed cooked tan-skinned sweet potatoes
⅔ cup chopped walnuts
⅔ cup dried cranberries

Cream cheese frosting:
1 stick butter, softened
1 (8-ounce) package cream cheese
1 (16-ounce) box powdered sugar, sifted
1 teaspoon vanilla extract

Preheat oven 350°F. Butter and flour 2 (9-inch) cake pans. Sift together flour, baking powder, baking soda, cinnamon, ginger, salt and cloves into a medium bowl. In a large bowl, combine oil and white and brown sugars; whisk until smooth. Whisk in eggs, 1 at a time. Mix in potatoes. Stir in flour mixture in 3 additions. Stir in nuts and cranberries. Pour batter into pans. Bake for about 30 minutes, or until a toothpick inserted in center comes out clean. Cool cakes completely. Frost between cake layers using ¾ cup of frosting, then frost top and sides of cake with remaining frosting. Chill for at least 2 hours before slicing and serving.

For the frosting: Beat butter and cream cheese. Beat in powdered sugar and vanilla until combined and smooth.

Fuquay Mineral Spring Inn

The Fuquay Mineral Spring Inn & Garden is a Colonial Revival home listed as a local landmark in Wake County. The inn is located directly across the street from the historic Fuquay Mineral Spring Park and is convenient to Raleigh-Durham, Cary, Fayetteville and Chapel Hill, as well as such attractions as Exploris, Alltel Pavilion, Raven Rock State Park, the Carolina Hurricanes hockey team and more.

The inn is perched on a hill overlooking the spring and has a garden with a period gazebo offering great views of the town of Fuquay-Varina.

INNKEEPERS: John & Patty Byrne
ADDRESS: 333 South Main Street
                  Fuquay-Varina, North Carolina 27526
TELEPHONE: (919) 552-3782; (866) 552-3782
E-MAIL: jbyrne@fuquayinn.com
WEBSITE: www.fuquayinn.com
ROOMS: 3 Rooms; 1 Suite; Private baths
CHILDREN: Children age 12 and older welcome
ANIMALS: Not allowed
HANDICAPPED: Not handicapped accessible
DIETARY NEEDS: Will accommodate guests' special dietary needs

Caribbean Crème Brûlée

Makes 6 Servings

1	cup heavy cream
1	cup fresh or canned coconut milk
8	egg yolks
⅓	cup plus 12 teaspoons sugar
1	teaspoon vanilla extract
½	cup dark rum
3	tablespoons sweetened flaked coconut, toasted

Preheat oven to 300°F. In a large bowl, combine cream, coconut milk, egg yolks, ⅓ cup of sugar, vanilla and rum; whisk until smooth (skim any foam or bubbles that may appear). Divide mixture among 6 individual ramekins or oven-proof custard cups. Put ramekins in a baking pan filled with 1-inch of hot water. Bake about for 40-50 minutes, until set around edges, but still a little loose in center. Remove from oven and let ramekins cool to room temperature in water bath. Remove ramekins from water bath and chill for at least 2 hours.

When ready to serve, sprinkle about 2 teaspoons of sugar over each crème brûlée. With a kitchen torch or under a preheated broiler, brown tops of crème brûlées until sugar has hardened (if using a kitchen torch, be careful as this custard contains alcohol which could cause the sugar to spatter from the flame). Sprinkle toasted coconut over crème brûlées and serve.

Earthshine Mountain Lodge

Call it a family resort, a guest ranch, a country inn, a mountain getaway or a bed & breakfast, Earthshine Mountain Lodge, south of Asheville and near Brevard, is unforgettable. This story-and-a-half, hand-built cedar log lodge opens to one of the finest views in eastern America. Magnificent rock fireplaces, patchwork quilts, stained glass lamps and log beds and rockers add to the mountain feel.

This 70-acre "grandmother's farm" borders Pisgah National Forest and is lovingly built upon a 100-year-old homestead.

INNKEEPERS:	Kim Heinitsh & Marion Boatwright
ADDRESS:	Route 1, Box 216-C
	Lake Toxaway, North Carolina 28747
TELEPHONE:	(828) 862-4207
E-MAIL:	earthshine@citcom.net
WEBSITE:	www.earthshinemtnlodge.com
ROOMS:	10 Rooms; 3 Suites; Private baths
CHILDREN:	Welcome
ANIMALS:	Not allowed; Resident sheep, goats & horses
HANDICAPPED:	Handicapped accessible
DIETARY NEEDS:	Will accommodate guests' special dietary needs

Chocolate Marble Cheesecake

Makes 1 Cake

"So light and fluffy, it will melt in your mouth." ~ Innkeeper, Earthshine Mountain Lodge

Crust:
2½   cups graham cracker crumbs
½   stick butter or margarine, melted
¾   cup sugar

Filling:
6   (8-ounce) packages cream cheese, softened
1¾   cups sugar
5   eggs
2   egg yolks
5   tablespoons all-purpose flour
½   cup heavy cream
1½   teaspoons vanilla extract
3   tablespoons chocolate sauce (or chocolate syrup)

For the crust: Thoroughly combine crust ingredients and press in bottom of a 10-inch springform pan.

For the filling: Preheat oven to 350°F. Beat cream cheese with a mixer until fluffy. Beat in sugar a little at a time. Beat in eggs, 1 at a time. Beat in egg yolks. Beat in flour, 1 tablespoon at a time. Add cream and vanilla; mix well (do not overmix).

Spread cream cheese mixture over crust. Drizzle with chocolate sauce and swirl with a toothpick. Bake for 1 hour. Remove from oven and cool, then chill and serve.

Corner Oak Manor

The Corner Oak Manor offers several weekend packages. The Women's Retreat Weekend includes a day at the spa with heated neck wrap, lip and eye treatments, foot soaks, microdermabrasion facial and foot and hand massage!

Innkeeper Karen Spradley has a culinary degree and delights in making breakfast a special experience. Guests appreciate her love of cooking in such delectable entrées as four-cheese and herb quiche, mushroom Brie strata, orange croissants or buttermilk French toast with berry compote.

INNKEEPERS:	Karen & Andy Spradley
ADDRESS:	53 Saint Dunstans Road
	Asheville, North Carolina 28803
TELEPHONE:	(828) 253-3525; (888) 633-3525
E-MAIL:	info@corneroakmanor.com
WEBSITE:	www.corneroakmanor.com
ROOMS:	3 Rooms; 1 Cottage; Private baths
CHILDREN:	Children age 12 and older welcome
ANIMALS:	Not allowed
HANDICAPPED:	Not handicapped accessible
DIETARY NEEDS:	Will accommodate guests' special dietary needs

Fudge Cappuccino Brownies

Makes 24 Servings

1½	sticks butter, softened
4	(1-ounce) squares unsweetened chocolate, chopped
1¾	cups sugar
1	tablespoon instant coffee powder
1½	teaspoons vanilla extract
1	cup all-purpose flour
½	teaspoon salt
1	teaspoon cinnamon
¼	teaspoon freshly grated nutmeg
3	large eggs, lightly beaten
1	cup semi-sweet chocolate chips

Preheat oven to 350°F. Spray a 9x13-inch baking pan with non-stick cooking spray. Melt butter and chocolate in a small saucepan over medium-low heat, stirring until smooth. Remove from heat and stir in sugar, coffee powder and vanilla.

In a large bowl, combine flour, salt, cinnamon and nutmeg. Add chocolate mixture and eggs; stir until blended. Fold in chocolate chips. Pour batter into pan. Bake for 30 minutes. Cool completely on a wire rack, then slice and serve.

1900 Inn on Montford

Elegantly furnished with English and American antiques dating from 1730 to 1910, the 1900 Inn on Montfort has four large guest rooms and a secluded, five-room, 1,000-square-foot third floor suite. Each room has a fireplace and three rooms have a whirlpool bath.

Breakfast is served in the formal dining room with a fruit course, a savory course such as baked tomatoes filled with eggs and Brie, shirred eggs or raspberry-filled French toast, and a dessert course, such as oven Danish, Bavarian puff pancakes or caramel pecan rolls.

INNKEEPERS:	Ron & Lynn Carlson
ADDRESS:	296 Montford
	Asheville, North Carolina 28801
TELEPHONE:	(828) 254-9569; (800) 254-9569
E-MAIL:	info@innonmontford.com
WEBSITE:	www.innonmontford.com
ROOMS:	4 Rooms; 1 Suite; Private baths
CHILDREN:	Children age 12 and older welcome
ANIMALS:	Not allowed; Resident cat
HANDICAPPED:	Not handicapped accessible
DIETARY NEEDS:	Will accommodate guests' special dietary needs

Lemon Angel Pie

Makes 6 to 8 Servings

Plan ahead, this pie needs to be chilled for at least 12 hours before serving.

Meringue shell:
4   egg whites
¼   teaspoon cream of tartar
1   cup sugar

Lemon filling:
4   egg yolks
¾   cup sugar
1   tablespoon all-purpose flour
½   cup water
Juice and grated zest of 1 lemon
1   cup whipping cream

For the meringue shell: Preheat oven to 275°F. Lightly butter an 8-inch pie pan. In a clean, dry bowl, beat egg whites and cream of tartar until foamy. Gradually add sugar, beating until egg whites form stiff peaks. Spread egg white mixture in pie pan. Bake for 90 minutes. Turn off oven; leave pan in oven until meringue is cool.

For the lemon filling: Combine egg yolks, sugar, flour, water, lemon juice and lemon zest in the top of a double boiler over very low heat; cook, stirring constantly, until thickened. Remove from heat and cool.

Twelve hours before serving, whip cream until stiff. Line meringue shell with ½ of whipped cream. Top with lemon filling. Top with remaining whipped cream. Chill for at least 12 hours, then slice and serve.

Note: The meringue shell may be prepared 1 day to 1 week ahead of time.

Cedar Crest Victorian Inn

The Cedar Crest Victorian Inn is in an ideal location, three blocks from the Biltmore Estate, just over a mile from downtown and four miles from the Blue Ridge Parkway. Four acres of towering trees, countless shades of green on terraced lawns and delightful flowering gardens adorn the inn.

Luxurious features in select rooms include Jacuzzi or grand claw-foot tubs and either gas or wood-burning fireplaces. Nightly turndown service affords the luxury of fluffed pillows with irresistible chocolates. And each morning, a breakfast feast is served in the dining room or on the spacious veranda.

INNKEEPERS:	Bruce & Rita Wightman
ADDRESS:	674 Biltmore Avenue
	Asheville, North Carolina 28803
TELEPHONE:	(828) 252-1389; (800) 252-0310
E-MAIL:	stay@cedarcrestvictorianinn.com
WEBSITE:	www.cedarcrestvictorianinn.com
ROOMS:	8 Rooms; 4 Suites; 1 Cottage; Private baths
CHILDREN:	Children age 10 and older welcome
ANIMALS:	Not allowed
HANDICAPPED:	Not handicapped accessible
DIETARY NEEDS:	Will accommodate guests' special dietary needs

Rhubarb Custard Pie

Makes 8 Servings

3   large eggs
1½   cups sugar
¼   cup all-purpose flour
½   teaspoon cinnamon
4   cups chopped (½-inch pieces) rhubarb
1   unbaked (9-inch) pie crust

Topping:
¾   cup all-purpose flour
¼   cup plus 2 tablespoons packed brown sugar
¾   stick butter, softened
¾   teaspoon cinnamon

Preheat oven to 400°F. In a medium bowl, beat eggs. In a small bowl, mix sugar, flour and cinnamon; stir into eggs. Stir in rhubarb. Pour filling into crust. Sprinkle topping over filling. Cover crust edges with foil and bake for 35 minutes. Remove foil and bake for 15 minutes more, or until done.

For the topping: Combine topping ingredients until crumbly.

The Duke Mansion

There is a long tradition of unforgettable hospitality at The Duke Mansion. Today the inn is dedicated to fine cuisine, remarkable service and beautiful presentation. With an emphasis on Southern charm in the Charlotte tradition, the chefs know how to add just the right flourish to make dining memorable.

Breakfast entrées may include banana pancakes with cranberry butter and maple syrup, eggs Benedict, smoked salmon and spinach quiche, shrimp and grits or coconut waffles with fruit compote and whipped cream.

INNKEEPERS:	The Lynnwood Foundation
ADDRESS:	400 Hermitage Road
	Charlotte, North Carolina 28207
TELEPHONE:	(704) 714-4400; (888) 202-1009
E-MAIL:	frontdesk@tlwf.com
WEBSITE:	www.dukemansion.org
ROOMS:	20 Rooms; Private baths
CHILDREN:	Welcome
ANIMALS:	Not allowed; Resident cats
HANDICAPPED:	Handicapped accessible
DIETARY NEEDS:	Will accommodate guests' special dietary needs

Strawberry & Sweet Cream Tart

Makes 4 Servings

1¼ cups all-purpose flour
3 tablespoons powdered sugar, divided plus extra, for garnish
7 tablespoons unsalted butter, softened
1 teaspoon lemon juice
Grated zest of 1 lemon
½ cup plus 2 tablespoons heavy cream
8 ounces strawberries, stemmed and quartered
4 tablespoons raspberry jelly
1 tablespoon water
4 sprigs fresh mint, for garnish

Preheat oven to 375°F. Sift together flour and 1½ tablespoons of powdered sugar into a medium bowl. Add butter and lemon juice; knead lightly until a smooth dough is formed. Cover bowl with plastic wrap and refrigerate for 15 minutes.

On a lightly floured surface, roll out dough thinly. Cut dough into 4 pieces. Line 4 (3-inch) tartlet pans with removable bottoms with dough. Put a piece of parchment paper and some dry beans over each piece of dough and bake for 15 minutes (this is called "baking blind"). Remove beans and parchment paper from crusts and bake for 3-5 minutes more, until crusts are golden brown. Cool for 15 minutes, then remove crusts from pans.

Whip cream, remaining 1½ tablespoons of powdered sugar and lemon zest until soft peaks are formed. Spoon whipped cream into crusts. Top with strawberries. Heat jelly with water in a small saucepan over low heat until jelly is melted and combined. Strain jelly mixture through a sieve and cool slightly. Spoon jelly mixture over strawberries to glaze. Dust with powdered sugar and garnish with a sprig of mint to serve.

Morehead Manor

A place where elegance, excitement and hospitality meet, the Morehead Manor Bed & Breakfast has four spacious guest rooms, each with a private bath. The Magnolia Suite has a king-size bed with a sitting area. The Eagle's Inn has two full-size beds and features a seven-head shower.

Morehead Manor is just moments from Duke University, North Carolina Central University, Research Triangle Park, RDU International Airport and is easily accessible to Interstates 85 and 40.

INNKEEPERS:	Daniel & Monica Edwards
ADDRESS:	914 Vickers Avenue
	Durham, North Carolina 27701
TELEPHONE:	(919) 687-4366; (888) 437-6333
E-MAIL:	info@moreheadmanor.com
WEBSITE:	www.moreheadmanor.com
ROOMS:	3 Rooms; 1 Suite; Private baths
CHILDREN:	Children age 12 and older welcome
ANIMALS:	Not allowed; Resident cat
HANDICAPPED:	Not handicapped accessible
DIETARY NEEDS:	Will accommodate guests' special dietary needs

Blueberry Delight

Makes 6 to 8 Servings

"A yummy summertime dessert that's cool and light." ~ Innkeeper, Morehead Manor Bed & Breakfast

Crust:
1   cup all-purpose flour
½   cup packed brown sugar
1   stick butter or margarine, melted
1   cup chopped pecans

Filling:
1   (8-ounce) package cream cheese
¾   cup sugar
1   teaspoon vanilla extract
1   (9-ounce) container Cool Whip

Topping:
1   pint fresh blueberries (frozen can be used)
1   cup sugar
1   tablespoon cornstarch
1   teaspoon lemon juice

For the crust: Preheat oven to 350°F. Combine crust ingredients and pat over bottom of a 9x13-inch baking dish. Bake for 10-15 minutes, then remove from oven and cool thoroughly.

For the filling: Blend filling ingredients thoroughly and spread over crust.

For the topping: Mix blueberries and sugar in a medium saucepan over medium heat. Bring to a boil. Mix cornstarch with a small amount of water until smooth, then stir into blueberry mixture. Stir in lemon juice. Lower heat and simmer until thickened. Cool, then pour over filling. Chill for at least 2 hours before serving.

Geographical Listing of Bed & Breakfasts

Alphabetical Listing of Bed & Breakfasts

Index

About the Author

Melissa Craven was the oldest child in a career Air Force family. She lived in the Tidewater, Virginia area for four years, which was the longest time she ever called a base home. Because of her childhood travels, Melissa was introduced to a variety of culinary styles. As an adult, she is not afraid to try new things in the kitchen. With a background in journalism, recipe testing, marketing and public relations she understands the need for clear and concise recipes. As a cook, she understands the joy that comes from creating a memorable meal for family and friends. Her melding of the two help create a winning recipe. Melissa is also the author of the Colorado Farmers' Market Cookbook and a contributing editor to each of the other books in the Bed & Breakfast Cookbook Series. Melissa now lives with her husband, Chad, and their black and chocolate labs in Denver, Colorado.

The Bed & Breakfast Cookbook Series

Entertain with ease and flair! B&B's and Country Inns from across the nation share their best and most requested recipes.

California Bed & Breakfast Cookbook
127 California B&B's and Country Inns. Book #5 in the series.
$19.95 / 328pp / ISBN 1-889593-11-7

Colorado Bed & Breakfast Cookbook
88 Colorado B&B's and Country Inns. Book #1 in the series. New 2nd ed!
$19.95 / 320pp / ISBN 0-9653751-0-2

New England Bed & Breakfast Cookbook
107 B&B's and Country Inns in CT, MA, ME, NH, RI & VT. Book #6.
$19.95 / 320pp / ISBN 1-889593-12-5

North Carolina Bed & Breakfast Cookbook
62 North Carolina B&B's and Country Inns. Book #7 in the series. New!
$19.95 / 320pp / ISBN 1-889593-08-7

Texas Bed & Breakfast Cookbook
70 Texas B&B's, Guest Ranches and Country Inns. Book #3 in the series.
$19.95 / 320pp / ISBN 1-889593-07-9

Virginia Bed & Breakfast Cookbook
94 Virginia B&B's and Country Inns. Book #4 in the series. New 2nd ed.
$19.95 / 320pp / ISBN 1-889593-04-1

Washington State Bed & Breakfast Cookbook
72 Washington B&B's and Country Inns. Book #2 in the series. New 2nd ed!
$19.95 / 320pp / ISBN 1-889593-05-2

❧ Coming Soon: *Georgia, New York & Pennsylvania* (Spring, 2006). ❧

Bed & Breakfast Cookbook Series
Order Form

2969 Baseline Road, Boulder CO 80303
888.456.3607 • www.3dpress.net • orders@3dpress.net

PLEASE SEND ME:	Price	Quantity
CALIFORNIA BED & BREAKFAST COOKBOOK	$19.95	_____
COLORADO BED & BREAKFAST COOKBOOK	$19.95	_____
NEW ENGLAND BED & BREAKFAST COOKBOOK	$19.95	_____
NORTH CAROLINA BED & BREAKFAST COOKBOOK	$19.95	_____
TEXAS BED & BREAKFAST COOKBOOK	$19.95	_____
VIRGINIA BED & BREAKFAST COOKBOOK	$19.95	_____
WASHINGTON STATE BED & BREAKFAST COOKBOOK	$19.95	_____

SUBTOTAL: $ _____

Colorado residents add 3.8% sales tax. Denver residents add 7.2% $ _____

Add $5.00 for shipping for 1st book, add $1 for each additional $ _____

TOTAL ENCLOSED: $ _____

*Special offer: Buy any 2 books in the series and take a 10% discount.
Buy any 4 or more books and take a 25% discount!

SEND TO:

Name_____

Address _____

City _____State _____Zip _____

Phone_____A gift from: _____

We accept checks, money orders, Visa or Mastercard. Please make checks payable to 3D Press, Inc.

Please charge my   ☐ VISA   ☐ MASTERCARD

Card Number _____Expiration Date _____

The Bed & Breakfast Cookbook Series

Entertain with ease and flair! B&B's and Country Inns from across the nation share their best and most requested recipes.

California Bed & Breakfast Cookbook
127 California B&B's and Country Inns. Book #5 in the series.
$19.95 / 328pp / ISBN 1-889593-11-7

Colorado Bed & Breakfast Cookbook
88 Colorado B&B's and Country Inns. Book #1 in the series. New 2nd ed!
$19.95 / 320pp / ISBN 0-9653751-0-2

New England Bed & Breakfast Cookbook
107 B&B's and Country Inns in CT, MA, ME, NH, RI & VT. Book #6.
$19.95 / 320pp / ISBN 1-889593-12-5

North Carolina Bed & Breakfast Cookbook
62 North Carolina B&B's and Country Inns. Book #7 in the series. New!
$19.95 / 320pp / ISBN 1-889593-08-7

Texas Bed & Breakfast Cookbook
70 Texas B&B's, Guest Ranches and Country Inns. Book #3 in the series.
$19.95 / 320pp / ISBN 1-889593-07-9

Virginia Bed & Breakfast Cookbook
94 Virginia B&B's and Country Inns. Book #4 in the series. New 2nd ed.
$19.95 / 320pp / ISBN 1-889593-04-1

Washington State Bed & Breakfast Cookbook
72 Washington B&B's and Country Inns. Book #2 in the series. New 2nd ed!
$19.95 / 320pp / ISBN 1-889593-05-2

✿ Coming Soon: *Georgia, New York & Pennsylvania* (Spring, 2006). ✿

Bed & Breakfast Cookbook Series
Order Form

2969 Baseline Road, Boulder CO 80303
888.456.3607 • www.3dpress.net • orders@3dpress.net

PLEASE SEND ME:	Price	Quantity
CALIFORNIA BED & BREAKFAST COOKBOOK	$19.95	_____
COLORADO BED & BREAKFAST COOKBOOK	$19.95	_____
NEW ENGLAND BED & BREAKFAST COOKBOOK	$19.95	_____
NORTH CAROLINA BED & BREAKFAST COOKBOOK	$19.95	_____
TEXAS BED & BREAKFAST COOKBOOK	$19.95	_____
VIRGINIA BED & BREAKFAST COOKBOOK	$19.95	_____
WASHINGTON STATE BED & BREAKFAST COOKBOOK	$19.95	_____

SUBTOTAL: $ _____

Colorado residents add 3.8% sales tax. Denver residents add 7.2% $ _____

Add $5.00 for shipping for 1st book, add $1 for each additional $ _____

TOTAL ENCLOSED: $ _____

*Special offer: Buy any 2 books in the series and take a 10% discount.
Buy any 4 or more books and take a 25% discount!

SEND TO:

Name_____

Address _____

City _____ State _____ Zip _____

Phone_____ A gift from: _____

We accept checks, money orders, Visa or Mastercard. Please make checks payable to 3D Press, Inc.

Please charge my   ☐ VISA   ☐ MASTERCARD

Card Number _____ Expiration Date _____